Edwardian Album

Nicolas Bentley

# Edwardian Album

## A Photographic Excursion into
## a Lost Age of Innocence

Photographic research by
Andra Nelki

CARDINAL edition published in 1974
by Sphere Books Ltd
30/32 Gray's Inn Road
London WC1X 8JL

Published simultaneously in hardback by
Weidenfeld & Nicolson Ltd
11 St John's Hill
London SW11

Introduction copyright © 1974 by Nicolas Bentley

ISBN 0 351 15304 7

Designed by Trevor Vincent
Filmset by Keyspools Ltd, Golborne, Lancs
Printed by Tinling (1973) Ltd, Prescot and London

# Contents

*Introduction by Nicolas Bentley* . 9

Domestic Bliss . . . . . . 63

Unwillingly to School . . . 79

Travels and Excursions . . . 93

Below Stairs . . . . . . 107

London Life . . . . . . 123

A Nation of Shopkeepers . . . 145

In the Country . . . . . . 159

The Seaside . . . . . . 173

The Sporting Life . . . . 185

The Beginning of the End . . 207

*Bibliography* . . . . . . 217

*Photographic Acknowledgements* . 219

*Index* . . . . . . . 221

# Edwardian Album

This unique album of photographs and Nicolas Bentley's
fascinating text vividly recreate the everyday world of
Edwardian England: architecture and scenery; great
occasions and scenes of humble domesticity; elegant
celebrities and the all too numerous poor. The illustrations
have been chosen from the wealth of photographic material
which exists both in public and family collections, much of
which has never previously been reproduced.

The jacket design is based on the cover of an Edwardian photographic
album belonging to Cecilia Willes. The photographs are from the
collections of P. H. Frisby (front) and Kevin MacDonnell (back).

# Introduction

BY NICOLAS BENTLEY

It is not easy to find the *mot juste* for the Edwardian era. By comparison with the reigns of most of his predecessors, King Edward's reign was short; it lasted only nine years and it is difficult to point to anything that happened during those years that could be said to have had dramatic or far-reaching consequences on the destinies of the British people. The split in the Conservative party over Tariff Reform and the resulting triumph of the Liberals; the intractable question of Ireland; the Education Act of 1902; and the clash between the Commons and the Lords over the Parliament Bill, by which their lordships' talons were to be clipped; the advent of the Suffragettes – these were events which, though they loomed large at the time, were hardly on the scale of those cataclysmic changes that had characterized the reigns of so many preceding sovereigns. There were no blood-drenched dynastic squabbles, no major wars of aggression (discounting Britain's predatory excursions into Africa), no bold resistance to a foreign invader. There was no clash between Church and State, no fundamental challenge to authority. In spite of the political traumas of the period, it was an era of peace, prosperity and self-satisfaction.

There is a useful elasticity in the term 'era'. To try to restrict its meaning to the precise period of King Edward's reign would be pedantic and illogical. A literal interpretation of the Edwardian era would obscure significant causes at one end of the period and omit their effects at the other. So here from time to time the shadow either of Queen Victoria or of George v may be seen to fall across the page.

But first a word of warning: it should not be assumed that what follows aspires to the category of history. Call it rather a commentary on the social scene, and if occasionally the shrill, assertive voice of politics intrudes itself or if there are fleeting murmurs about economics, such sounds are introduced only to enlarge the perspective of the scene.

The Edwardians were preoccupied largely with the present and the immediate past. The future was only to be seen dimly through a haze that promised continued fine weather. Imagination still glowed with those ideals of Empire that had fired the hearts and commercial instincts of the late Victorians, those fights for the flag in which Wolseley, Roberts, Kitchener and Buller had shown those of lesser breeds the innate superiority of the Britisher.

It was in this balmy climate of self-esteem that the Edwardians went their various ways. That the *status quo* was ever likely to be drastically interfered with was not a possibility that anyone could take seriously, except a few crackpots like Bernard Shaw (and what would you expect of a vegetarian atheist?) or H.G. Wells, a little counter-jumper with a squeaky voice.

And yet, not for the first time in history, the crackpots, as events proved, were not so far out in their predictions. For in time's long-distance lens we see the Edwardian era as no more than a hiatus between the golden apogee of Victorian omnipotence and grandeur and the evaporation of its residue

The exploits of Wolseley, Roberts and Kitchener caused many a fight for the flag to be re-enacted on British soil.

Bernard Shaw, the leading anti-establishment figure of the day. His views on moral, social and political questions, expressed with characteristic irony, often produced an unsightly rash on the complacent face of Society.

before the twentieth century had run half its course.

Four years after King Edward's reign the first steps towards decline had accelerated to a gallop. Already, while the King was still alive, the sound of those steps was audible to those who kept their ears to the ground. They were sounds that proclaimed, not the immediate end of the old order, but unmistakably the beginning of the end. And when the end came, it was, as J.B.Morton has described it, 'the end of a careless light-heartedness. One came to manhood through a terrible gate, and suddenly, without the preparation that had been expected. Boy-hood, in those days, did not pass quietly into manhood, but was rent away in a gun-flash and departed for ever in a single night of violence.'

It was a harsh and demoralizing experience and no section of the community escaped its repercussions. But in proportion to its num-bers there was one section that was perhaps harder hit than the rest, and that was what might have been described by any journalist

of the period as the flower of Edwardian youth. It is arguable that history might well have taken a different turn, leading to a pleasanter prospect than that which confronts the world today, if those resources of

In his *Barrack-room Ballads* Rudyard Kipling spoke eloquently about the drudgery of life in the army, but said nothing of the private soldier's dream world of pin-ups, with never a sergeant-major in sight.

intelligence and imagination, vision, enterprise and wisdom – with which the rising generation of Edwardians was well endowed – had not been so freely bespattered over the fields of Flanders.

Although hardly more than sixty years – roughly the span of Queen Victoria's reign – separates us, approaching the last quarter of the twentieth century, from the Edwardians, the distance between their era and our own seems in some ways as immense as the gulf that separated them from the Tudors. The benefits by which our own society is en-riched, however much we may squander or misuse them, and the inequalities and self-imposed handicaps by which our society is disfigured, were as little dreamt of in Edwardian days as their own brand of Liberalism, their industrial and commercial systems, their hansom cabs and music halls, were unimaginable to the Elizabethans. What were they like, then, these strange Edwardian ancestors of ours, so near and yet so far from

Jimmy Glover, the famous musical director of Drury Lane Theatre, who epitomised the vulgarity and flamboyance of Edwardian showbiz.

'Easy as winking', said the instructions. But was it?

the world of today, from life as it is led by their neo-Elizabethan descendants?

A truthful answer must be full of the contradictions that exist in the national character, as they exist in each of us individually. Not all those contradictions are always captured by the camera, but the camera's fidelity to nature, and especially human nature, is often closer than that which is expressed by other more partial observers; closer than the rhetoric of politicians, the evidence of statistics or opinion polls, the theories of sociologists or the reports of journalists. It is the camera's answer that is given here to the question: what were the Edwardians really like? It was only in their day, with the invention of cameras that were relatively cheap and easy to handle, that photography began to come into its own as a popular amusement. Until then it had been a cumbersome and rather expensive process for which an elaborate apparatus was needed, as well as a considerable amount of patience. A few Victorian pioneers – Fox Talbot, Julia Cameron and D.O. Hill among the best known – had shown what could be achieved by a camera in the

Photography was still something of a novelty and had its problems even for the experts, as well as its mysteries for the uninitiated.

hands of a sensitive and intelligent photographer. But more often it had been used to produce those little sepia portraits, stiff in their poses and unsmiling in their expressions, that filled so many family albums – portraits of bushy-whiskered father-figures, stern matriarchs, pale young curates, demure young women, yeomanry officers posing with their helmets on plaster columns, forgotten uncles and unwanted aunts. Progress towards cheaper and easier methods of photography had extended the camera's possibilities far beyond the comparatively limited use that the Victorians had made of it. To their obvious delight the Edwardians found themselves able to record not only each other's appearances, but also the appearance of their everyday world: its architecture and scenery in town and in the country; its citizens and its urban types; its elegant celebrities and its all too numerous underprivileged; events indoors and out of doors; state occasions and scenes of humble domesticity. The photographs in this book have been chosen from the vast amount of such material that exists in either public collections or in private hands, many in this last category being shown here for the first time.

Inevitably, mass production had its effect on quality. The care for pictorial arrangement, lighting and focus that characterized the work of the best Victorian photographers meant comparatively little to the Edwardian amateur, whose aim more often was a quick likeness or impression, the virtue of which was its immediacy. Such photographs were the forerunners of today's pictures in the press, which are meant merely to record the fleeting moment.

A fair proportion of these photographs will be seen to be of the middle class. There is no special significance in this, no implied emphasis on middle class virtues or shortcomings. It is simply that the middle class was more often photographed than either the leisured gentry, to whom photography as an amusement lacked the cachet of hunting, shooting and other expensive pastimes, or the poor to whom a hobby relatively so expensive as photography was far out of reach.

The middle class, that massive but amorphous entity, is one of those many Victorian inventions, such as the omnibus or public libraries or teetotalism, that occurred as an indirect consequence of the Industrial Revolution. Though innocuous in itself, the middle class was an off-shoot of one of the less attractive features of that Revolution – the aristocracy of wealth to which it gave rise. It was an aristocracy as acutely conscious of its situation as any of the landed gentry and was as determined as they were to preserve its privileges. It was with genuine awe that the Victorian middle class looked on the true blue-blooded aristocracy, but on the aristocracy of wealth it cast a covetous eye. For the hope of riches was easier to entertain than the hope of being ennobled, and members of the aristocracy were consequently revered as symbols of a charmed circle as enviable as it was elusive.

This instinctive respect for the hierarchy of the social system was transmitted more or less intact to the Edwardians. The hideous spectre of red revolution, inherent, for example, in the existence of trade unions, and the still more ghastly mutterings of a politically-minded minority infected with the Continental virus of republicanism, were portents of which the Edwardian middle class was well aware – though such perils were not so obtrusive as to cause serious concern. An unshakable faith in the permanence of the *status quo* and a complacency as stolid as that which had enveloped their fathers and grandfathers enveloped the Edwardian middle class as snugly as the furs bought by middle-class ladies at Swears and Wells or the mantles they bought at Jay's. And this complacency was reinforced by a consciousness that Britain had at its command the huge potential of the Empire, whose free-flowing resources of raw materials and cheap labour were the envy of other less fortunate and less deliberately acquisitive nations. The time was as rich in promise as it was in euphoria.

All classes, in spite of their acquiescing in a social system that kept each of them firmly in the station assigned to it by tradition or wealth, felt in varying degrees a sense of

Miss Zena Dare, swingin' along.

relief at being liberated from some of the more oppressive and out-dated conventions of the Victorian era. The power of the Church as a truly dominant force in society had begun, if almost imperceptibly, to diminish. Court circles were no longer quite as stuffy as in the Queen's day (though still stuffy enough). No longer was the stage a 'disreputable' profession, though among the aristocracy an antiquated snobbery about it persisted. In 1911, when Lord Esher's son, the Honourable Maurice Brett, then a lieutenant-colonel in the Coldstream Guards, married the actress, Miss Zena Dare, he was obliged to resign his commission. The condemnation of his wife implied by the edict that made this necessary was not because she appeared in musical comedy – if she had been branded with intellectual aspirations by acting in plays by Ibsen or Shaw she would probably have been considered even further beyond the pale – it was

the mere fact of her being an actress.

In other directions, however, barriers less stupid or obnoxious were being overthrown. A wind of change was blowing through the groves of Academe. What Dame Edith Sitwell described as 'the chilblained, mittened musings of Matthew Arnold', and the cheaper philosophies of writers such as Tupper and Smiles, had long ago had their day and the novels such as those of Marie Corelli and Elinor Glyn, though daring, were no longer taboo.

But while the Edwardian world went about its business and pursued its pleasures under the cheerful illusion that Britain's insularity, both geographical and metaphorical, would continue, as far as anyone could tell, to give it strength and independence, the true picture of the situation looked rather different. Its colours were drab and its tones subdued. The position is summarized in Philip Magnus's biography of King Edward: 'The land's surface glowed with a splendour that suggested serenity, but seismic faults had developed below, and the Edwardian age is characterized by a rapidly accelerating process of economic, social and political disturbance.'

Those in the know must undoubtedly have been apprehensive, but there were few voices crying in the wilderness. In private the King may have expressed concern at the way things were developing, anxious no doubt about the truculent antics of his cousin Kaiser Wilhelm, but in public he maintained an appearance of nonchalance.

It was the nonchalance of an avuncular rather than a paternalistic figure. The King had about him an air of good-humoured detachment that could more readily be associated with a well liked uncle than with an affectionate father figure. It was not that he was not conscientious, punctilious even, in discharging the many and often tedious responsibilities of his position, but he was less suited by temperament to the role of a paterfamilias than to that of an elderly buck, in which he was certainly more true to himself.

To do the King justice it is necessary to compare the picture he presented to his subjects with that which has been revealed

King Edward and Queen Alexandra with the President of France,
M. Armand Fallières, at the White City Exhibition in 1908.

by time. The public took an intense interest in the King, both as an individual with appetites and feelings much like its own and as a symbol of sovereignty, for which, as an institution, there was a widespread and more or less uncritical regard. The ambivalence of the situation in a permissive society, in which, while the person of the sovereign is cherished, sovereignty as an abstract concept is regarded at best with tolerant scepticism, is the sort of compromise that makes the British character so hard for people of other races to understand. In the days of King Edward such a compromise could hardly have been expected. The British empire was still a going concern. It needed a titular boss and although the King's private character might not have been all that seemed desirable, his public presence and his partiality for the trappings of state were in line with the popular idea of what was requisite in the head of an empire.

The British people as a whole were, as they still are, much attached to such trappings, and although Edward's reputation was less than immaculate, this did not diminish the universal reverence that was felt for the Crown. But times have changed and the institution of monarchy is nowadays regarded by many as an anachronism in an age in which the enlightened policies and humanitarian conduct of the Soviet regime are seen as portents of a golden era of universal love and friendship.

In private life the King's behaviour was perhaps not all that the public would have liked or approved, but such behaviour was by no means exceptional in high society. Some of the small set that comprised his more intimate friends were unfaithful to their wives with those of other men like themselves. An affair with a woman not in society would have been as unthinkable as indecent exposure. The wives, acquiescent because they had no alternative — the creation of an outright scandal would have put an end to their position in society — took well-born lovers, not out of revenge, or seldom so, but out of boredom, curiosity, or in some cases genuine love.

A day at the races. In the paddock, the King's favourite, Miss Lillie Langtry.

Though outwardly the King remained a model of respectability his behaviour behind the scenes was often less than creditable. Again to quote Philip Magnus, '. . . the social code continued to allow the rich a privileged degree of latitude so long as public scandal was avoided'. As sometimes happens in societies that discard the simple moral codes of more primitive communities, appearances were held to be more important than reality. If the King neglected his patient, decorous consort in favour of a mistress or two, it was not thought to matter much, as long as his liaisons were conducted with discretion.

Discreet his amours may have been, yet somehow knowledge of them seemed to get abroad. It was not for their looks alone that the public stood on chairs in Hyde Park to gape at Mrs Keppel or Lillie Langtry riding in their carriages. Salacious visions of these and other ladies in the King's fat embrace assured them a fame that neither their beauty nor their talents would otherwise be likely to have achieved for them.

It is said that Queen Alexandra accepted the King's habitual infidelities not so much with resignation as with relief. At least they kept him out of her own bed and the exemplary patience and good humour that she showed in her undignified predicament made an edifying comparison with the King's lubricious pursuit of other women.

Though the public frequently turned a blind eye to Edward's extra-marital adventures – from personal experience or by some slight stretch of imagination a good many men or women could see themselves in the same situation – the public was less inclined to be charitable when the King's behaviour got him into difficulties which, if they had threatened an ordinary member of society, might well have had more serious consequences. In 1891, Edward, then Prince of Wales, was dragged into the Tranby Croft case, in which Sir William Gordon-Cumming, a colonel in the Scots Guards, was accused of cheating at cards. It was an unsavoury affair and there was a conspicuous lack of sympathy for the Prince. The embarrassment that he must have suffered at having to appear in the witness box and his grilling by the Solicitor-General, who appeared for the accused colonel, far from arousing feelings of commiseration engendered a suspicion that it served him right. If anyone less privileged had been caught playing an illegal game of baccarat there would almost certainly have been a prosecution.

If the public had known also about some of the puerile excesses of Edward's behaviour in private his popularity at this time might have slumped still further. Until he came to the throne, and possibly afterwards, his idea of a joke was likely to centre on horse-play. Christopher Sykes, an old and faithful lickspittle, who died only a few years before Edward became King, remained consistently loyal in circumstances to which no man less servile would have submitted. He was a large, lugubrious man, who seldom smiled and was therefore a ready-made butt. He accepted with stoic indifference the various indignities to which he was subjected, as when the Prince doused his head and beard with brandy, which became a stock joke, or fenced him in with cues under the billiard table. With equal equanimity he allowed himself to be used as a convenience and his house as a hotel, and when, having squandered a fortune on entertaining the Prince and his entourage, Sykes found himself teetering on the edge of bankruptcy, it was the Prince who felt himself ill-used.

Fortunately, such episodes were not widely known and except for the Tranby Croft case, which had occurred almost ten years earlier, by the time Edward came to the throne his image was one that the public on the whole was ready to accept without criticism. It was, after all, an image very like its own. The King paid lip service to the Church of England and in politics was a Conservative. His taste in the arts was philistine and his pleasures were conventional. Perhaps nothing endeared him more to the public than when his horses won the Derby, as they did in 1896, in 1900 and again in 1909. And if by reason of his position he was able to travel more widely and in considerably greater comfort than most people, he seemed to remain, except for a life-long attachment to *la vie Parisienne*, singularly unimpressed by what he saw and incurious about what he did not see.

The redeeming features of the King's nature, however, were as undeniable as they were obvious. He was above all an extrovert and would no more have thought of feigning sentiments he did not feel or beliefs that were not his than of insulting a guest at his own table. Nothing was more genuine than his inspiring personal loyalty and genuine friendship has been too widely recorded to be dismissed merely as sycophancy. The tact and kindness that he usually showed towards friends who were down on their luck, whether through gambling, illness, or some other misfortune, are also well known. Perhaps that odd and uncompromising character, 'Jacky' Fisher, who knew the King as well as any man, gave the truest summary of the appeal of his ambivalent personality when in writing about the King shortly after his death he declared that he 'conquered all hearts and annihilated all envy'.

In spite of his conscientiousness the King was on the whole indifferent to matters outside the range of his own experience, and it can hardly have encouraged him to interest himself in affairs of state to have been treated by Victoria as though he were mentally handicapped. It is to his credit that he nevertheless acquired not only a genuine understanding of the principles of constitutional government, but some idea of the sort of irrational prejudices by which public feeling is often swayed. But his interest in subjects or ideas that were beyond his immediate and somewhat limited knowledge was slight. His chief preoccupations in the line of duty were foreign affairs – domestic politics bored him – the Army and the Navy. When, as King, he began to take an active part in such subjects, he showed himself to be more dutiful than enlightened or original. Nor did this seem to be the sign of an intelligence sufficiently subtle to appreciate that monarchs who occasionally reveal unsuspected depths of wisdom are likely to be regarded with suspicion by their ministers. Edward on coming to the throne showed, however, that the long period spent waiting in the wings had not been entirely wasted. In their assessment of his abilities, Hugh Chisholm, who was for long associated with *The Times* of London, and Lord Esher, a close friend and adviser of the King, remarked that 'While Prince of Wales he had a widespread knowledge of public affairs, but little training in statecraft. When he became King his genuine capacity for affairs was a matter of general surprise.

King Edward, with the Prince of Wales (*right*), later King George V, at his last Derby in 1909. The winner was the King's horse, Minoru.

sense of duty, in spite of all that Queen Victoria had done to try and stunt it, while complaining at the same time that the Prince lacked responsibility. Had she allowed him an opportunity to display that sense, she would no doubt have been surprised. His firm and reasoned belief, for instance, in the principles of the Entente Cordiale and his efforts towards its achievement won him considerable respect and admiration in France as well as in England. His capacity for

Among the King's pastimes was shooting. Under his careful supervision the number of heads of game shot annually on the royal estates at Sandringham in Norfolk, rose from 7,000 to some 30,000.

It was his ministers, however, rather than the general public by whom this surprise was chiefly felt, though the public would no doubt have been equally surprised had it been aware of the enthusiasm and determination with which Edward embarked on his new role of King.

It is easier nowadays for the sovereign to keep in touch with public feeling than it was in those days. The media had not yet arrogated the high responsibility that once belonged to Parliament – the responsibility of assessing public opinion on the fundamental issues of the day and interpreting its strength. Edward, as King, was dependent therefore to a large extent on his ministers' views as to what the public might be thinking or saying. But how well informed were they, the ministers themselves? And what sort of men were they, who had the responsibility of guiding the nation's affairs and who held to a very considerable degree the public's destiny in their own hands?

Of the four prime ministers who served the King, the first, the Marquess of Salisbury (1901–02) and the second, his nephew, A. J. Balfour (later the Earl of Balfour) (1902–05), were Conservative, aristocratic old Etonians, and both were equally far removed from contact with the electorate. The other two, both Liberals, were Sir Henry Campbell-Bannerman (1905–08) and Mr Asquith (later the Earl of Oxford and Asquith) (1908–10). Although of humbler origins than their predecessors, both of them,

The Marquess of Salisbury, Prime Minister in 1901–02. He was a shrewd and experienced parliamentarian of the old school, as well as a skilful diplomat; but his long career was drawing to its close by the time Edward became King.

Sir Henry Campbell-Bannerman, the great nonentity of Edwardian politics, was Prime Minister from 1905 until 1908. He is remembered chiefly as the man about whom all is forgotten.

Lord Salisbury was succeeded as Prime Minister by the Rt Hon. A. J. Balfour (later the Earl of Balfour). The King was decidedly antipathetic to his scholarly turn of mind and distant courtesy.

The Rt Hon. H. H. Asquith (later the Earl of Oxford and Asquith), Prime Minister from 1908 until the King's death in 1910. Sir Winston Churchill, who served in Asquith's cabinet, remarked that 'vast knowledge, faithful industry, deep thought were embedded in his nature'.

by upbringing and natural inclination, were equally far removed from direct contact with the masses.

Lord Salisbury's period as prime minister was the shortest; too short to allow much of his wisdom and experience to brush off on the King, just as Lord Melbourne's period of benign tutelage had been too short to give the young Victoria more than an elementary grounding in the role of a constitutional sovereign. Salisbury was perhaps the most outstanding of the King's four prime ministers. He had played a notable part in the settlement of various crises through which one European country or another had staggered during the latter half of Queen Victoria's reign, and the public had chalked it up as a mark in his favour that he disliked and distrusted Bismarck, whose dubious achievement in unifying the Germanic states had been off-set by his arrogant and devious conduct of affairs.

Salisbury was succeeded after eighteen months by Arthur Balfour, with whom the King until then had had little to do. If he could have followed his inclinations they would no doubt have seen still less of each other. Balfour was a philosopher and an aesthete, a bachelor and an ascetic, all things anathema to the King, who, apart from state documents, seldom read anything except newspapers, unless perhaps it was to thumb his way through Ruff's *Guide to the Turf*. Balfour, more discreet and less unctuous than Disraeli (who presented a set of his novels to Queen Victoria) did not press his literary works on King Edward, and so posterity can only speculate on what might have been the King's opinion of *A Defence of Philosophy* or *The Foundations of Belief*.

Balfour's strength as a politician lay largely in his diplomatic skill and his experience as a negotiator. But from the beginning the King's mistrust of intellectuals put Balfour at a disadvantage. Though neither of them could ever have found the other congenial, Edward respected Balfour's integrity and whatever Balfour's private feelings about the King may have been, his attitude in discussion was invariably courteous and correct.

Winston Churchill (*above*), Home Secretary, and Lloyd George (*below*), Chancellor of the Exchequer, *les enfants terribles* of Edwardian politics. Though the ruling class tended to mistrust their radical ideas, the broad mass of the people usually supported them.

In spite of their fundamental differences of character and temperament there must have been some ambiguity in the King's feelings at parting from Balfour when in 1905 the Unionist government resigned. It was virtually certain that a Liberal government would take its place, and the word Liberal was decidedly obnoxious to the King. Moreover, the party's radicals, foremost among them Winston Churchill and Lloyd George, were objects of his particular dislike. It is fair to add, however, that time and experience served to modify the King's opinion of them both, though to begin with his mistrust, particularly of Lloyd George, had been profound.

Sir Henry Campbell-Bannerman was a man of more moderate views whom the King found it easier to get on with. The contrast between Balfour's aloof manner, conditioned by the glacial atmosphere of his wide-ranging intellect, and 'C-B's' jocular and somewhat earthy personality could hardly have been more marked. At first the King felt a sense of relief. But 'C-B' was getting on in years and before long his health began to fail. He had in any case none of the *finesse* that Balfour had shown in his relationship with the King. He was lax over keeping him informed about discussions in the cabinet and the relief which the King had felt at Balfour's retirement and 'C-B's' assumption of office soon gave way to querulous complaints about his once again being treated as a 'puppet'.

For several months before illness forced Campbell-Bannerman to retire, Asquith, the deputy prime minister, had been in charge of affairs. He had already shown himself extremely able as leader of the House of Commons; his genius for procrastination, which was a marked feature of the later stages of his political career, had not yet become an inhibiting factor. He was a man of powerful intellect, astute and incorruptible in his opinions; but in the King's view he suffered, like Balfour, from certain innate handicaps: his origins were middle-class, Nonconformist, and Liberal, and his interests, apart from politics, were intellectual. It was a bad start, but as the two got to know each other

better matters began to improve. The King's robust, if erratic, common sense appealed to the practical side of Asquith's nature, and as Keith Middlemas points out in his biography of the King, his antipathy towards the more progressive members of the cabinet no doubt influenced him to 'acceptance of Asquith as a check against radical policies likely, in his opinion, to damage the harmony of society and weaken national security'.

Most of the political issues and party struggles of King Edward's reign, struggles which racked MPs, reverberated throughout the press, and absorbed the interest of large sections of the public, have now dwindled into insignificance. Even the constitutional crisis over plans to reform the House of Lords, which overshadowed the last months of the King's reign, is now only of interest to historians and students of the period.

A crisis of a different kind, longer and more bitter than any other that arose, was precipitated by the demand that women should be allowed the vote. At this distance from events it is hard to believe that controversy over such an issue could have generated so much sound and fury; what now seems a just and natural prerogative then seemed – to many women as well as men – a shameful and even dangerous policy. The battle was perhaps the hardest fought, and in its consequences one of the most significant, by which Edwardian England was confronted.

It was largely owing to the blind prejudice and devious tactics of members of Parliament that women were denied the right to vote long after it had been widely accepted that the main arguments against their being allowed to do so were no longer valid. The claim of political expediency was about all that the politicians had to fall back on. It was claimed that votes for women would alter the composition of the electorate and hence the balance of the sexes. And there was no certainty about the way in which women – particularly unmarried women – might vote. The steady improvement in educational facilities for young women had engendered a new spirit of independence among them; some might even defy their parents or their husbands and vote according to beliefs of

Mrs Emmeline Pankhurst, the Demon Queen of what many people regarded as the Suffragettes' pantomime, expounding the case for female suffrage at a meeting in Trafalgar Square.

their own; not a reassuring prospect.

Votes for Women is said to have featured in the draft manifesto of the Chartist movement, drawn up in 1838, but the idea of their having enough sense to think for themselves and cast votes in a responsible manner was then thought too extravagant to be taken seriously and the proposal was apparently dropped in order to avoid bringing ridicule on the movement. In spite of this, a number of influential voices were later raised in favour of the proposal, among them Disraeli's, Cobden's and John Stuart Mill's. Now the idea was in the air again and many ladies who might become eligible for the vote would be able to remember with what respect their parents had spoken of one or another of these famous figures and to recall that all three of them had supported women's suffrage.

With backing so heterogeneous, yet at the same time so respectable, the cause from then on had begun to prosper and in a modest way had continued to do so against all opposition. By 1884, it began to look as though the battle might be nearing its end. A substantial number of MPs were by then in favour of votes for women and it was hoped that this end might be achieved by an amendment to the Reform Bill introduced in that year. Gladstone, never overtly a ladies' man, at first supported the idea, but when it came to the crunch he managed to find grounds for throwing the amendment overboard. But by now the question had become a national issue; it was obviously only a question of time before women got the vote. Meanwhile, beaks and claws were sharpened on both sides for the final battle.

In 1903, the Women's Social and Political Union was established under the capable, if somewhat dictatorial, leadership of Mrs Emmeline Pankhurst. The Union's members, who by a delicate whimsy on Lord Northcliffe's part came to be known as

Suffragettes, were mostly members of the middle class, for in spite of all the excitement over the issue it remained an unfortunate fact that since the elimination of Votes for Women from the Chartists' manifesto, the working class as a whole had been disappointingly apathetic.

Both Parliament and the press were at first inclined to play down the activities of the Suffragettes; if no one took any notice it was thought that perhaps they might go away. But Mrs Pankhurst was made of sterner stuff than had been expected. In 1908, by which time Asquith had replaced Campbell-Bannerman as prime minister, she decided to make her presence felt by adopting militant tactics. Her followers, some of them ladies of impeccable birth and character, began to chain themselves to the railings of public buildings; they screamed and shouted; they made scenes in Downing Street and outside Buckingham Palace, justifying the view of those who agreed with the King in condemning their behaviour as 'outrageous'; they also assaulted the police and got sent to prison for doing so; there they went on hunger strike and resisted attempts at forcible feeding with such violence that they had to be let out again.

Politicians were divided among themselves about the wisdom of giving in to Mrs Pankhurst and her supporters. But, as often happens in politics, self-interest took precedence over principle and instead of sinking their differences in a concerted attempt either to ward off the catastrophe or to make women's suffrage a glorious reality, various politicians pursued various lines of argument for or against the proposition. Asquith was luke-warm; Balfour was all in favour; Bonar Law, who found it hard work to show enthusiasm at any time, took a dismal view of things; Churchill shilly-shallied; Sir Edward Grey, too, couldn't make up his mind. Even the Labour party, which theoretically supported the Suffragettes' cause, found itself in some disarray when it came to the point of taking a hard line. A number of Labour MPs were afraid that to give the vote to certain categories of women might imperil the chances of attaining universal suffrage for

Mrs Elsie Drummond, one of the foremost – and most formidable – of the Suffragettes, who, like most of the movement's leaders, became a martyr to the cause through arrest and imprisonment.

Miss Elsie Howie, a canon's daughter and militant Suffragette, photographed in Holloway Gaol, where she was several times imprisoned.

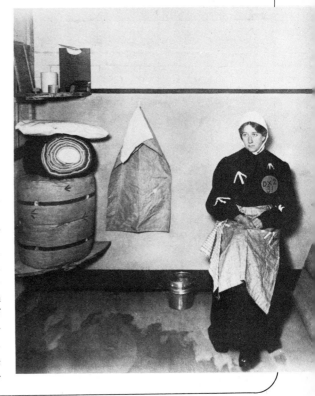

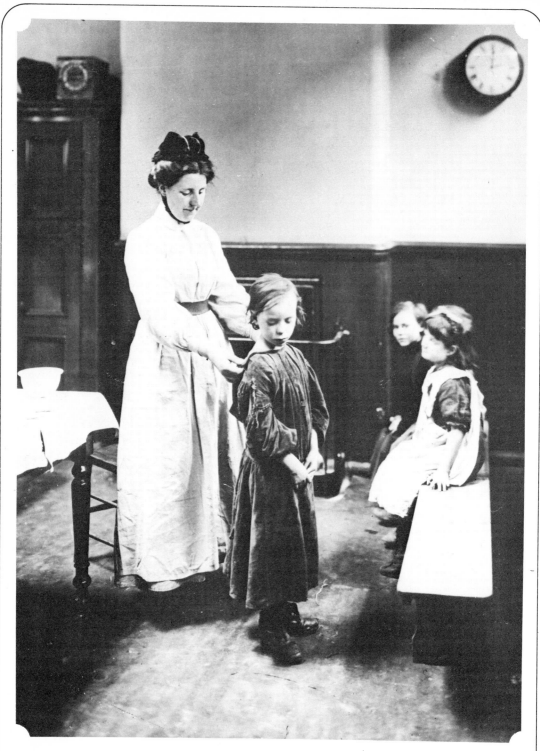

A pre-vision of the National Health service.
Systematic physical inspection helped to check
the dismal incidence of impetigo, ringworm,
lice and other endemic afflictions that were rife
among poor children.

men. One of the few leading politicians who was not afraid to risk his reputation was Lloyd George, who backed the Suffragettes. Predictably, his appearance at a meeting in the Albert Hall in their support scandalized the King, who thought it 'a most improper thing' for a member of the government to have done and complained to Asquith that 'it showed an entire absence of good judgement, good taste and propriety'. But Lloyd George remained unrepentant. In his view, either universal suffrage should be allowed both to men and women or there should be no change, for the enfranchisement of women on equal terms with men would mean a large increase in the middle class vote and traditionally the middle classes tended to vote Conservative.

Meanwhile, Mrs Pankhurst's cohorts continued to gather strength and by increasingly violent means – so violent that eventually their campaign of sabotage and disruption alienated even some of their warmest supporters – made themselves a permanent embarrassment to the government. The success of their efforts, though it was to be delayed by the First World War, was by this time inevitable and in 1918, after a struggle lasting more than fifteen years, Votes for Women, one of the most disagreeable and contentious issues of the Edwardian era, became a reality.

Discounting this embittered and unhappy phase of the King's reign, the impression of it that remains is that it was a period of haphazard development and *laissez faire* rather than systematic and co-ordinated progress. Health, housing, education, the welfare of the young, the old and the sick, tended each to be regarded as separate entities rather than as related and interdependent problems. The welfare state was as yet no more than a gleam in the eyes of a few idealists, though the need for some such apparatus was already obvious. But among the ruling class the will to introduce the necessary reforms was too half-hearted to be really effective and among the poor the attainment of real political power still lay a long way off.

In 1906, Sir Henry Campbell-Bannerman took office as the leader of a Liberal administration. The new government's domestic policies were at first not so very far in advance of those that had been promulgated by the Unionists under Mr Balfour. It was not until towards the end of King Edward's reign that the Liberals came to be regarded as eager apostles of social reform. Their watchword hitherto had been moderation. It was only when Lloyd George and Winston Churchill, self-appointed keepers of the Party's conscience, began to make their voices heard, that things noticeably began to change.

The inequalities between the rich and the poor, though much more apparent in their effects than those that exist nowadays, aroused remarkably little indiscipline and class hatred. The perpetuation of those inequalities was due partly to the working classes' lack of organization and partly to the vested interests of most landowners and employers in maintaining the *status quo*. But the churches, too, whose moral authority in those days still counted for something, were not without a share of responsibility for this state of affairs. Church leaders of various denominations, united only in their abhorrence of each other's dogma, showed a strange apathy towards problems of political morality.

The poverty and degradation that existed in the slums of London and other great cities, especially in the industrial centres, and among the huge numbers who worked on the land, were bemoaned by the Churches, High and Low; but the idea of their uniting in significant protest against the system that perpetuated such evils stank of the cesspit of ecumenicity. Better to be condemned for a lack of charity or even sincerity than to admit an identity of ideals with a sect whose creed offended against the orthodoxy of one's own. Prelates, priests and pastors thus remained isolated and for the most part discreetly silent. Though the terror of the stake which had not deterred Latimer or Ridley from sticking to their beliefs had long ago been exorcised, there was a noticeable disinclination among the higher clergy to commit themselves on social issues that might involve their having to stand up and be

To those whose consciences were alive to the situation, the circumstances of the leisured class, living in comfort and tranquillity, offered a disturbing comparison with the living conditions frequently suffered by the poor.

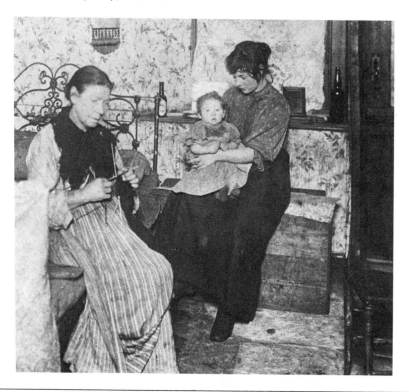

counted. Among the foremost religious leaders few raised their voices in public condemnation of either the principles or personalities involved in the continued existence of gross poverty and filthy slums.

Yet in other matters the influence of the churches was still considerable. Although religion was no longer the omnipotent force that it had been during much of the Victorian era, the formalities of religious observance were still adhered to by substantial sections of both the educated and the under-educated. Churches and chapels alike had large and loyal congregations and except in coteries of cranks, doubt or disbelief were regarded with much the same sort of feeling as nits or ringworm: an unfortunate occurrence that was not referred to if it cropped up in one's own family; a disgrace when it happened in someone else's.

If religion had lost a good deal of the mystical power it exerted in more superstitious times, the political influence of the established Church, through its adherents in both houses of Parliament, was still a force to be reckoned with. There could have been no messing about with the language of the Bible or variations of accepted ritual such as have been tolerated since. But more important was the moral authority of the church, whose approval or disapproval could contribute to the success or failure of an enterprise or the achievement or frustration of an ambition, perhaps even of a career, if that achievement or success required the acquiescence of society. But in other matters the established Church no longer had a monopoly of influence. The enfranchisement of the working class, completed by the passing of the Reform Bill of 1884, had given political power of a more realistic kind to a sizeable army of Nonconformists, whose views on most matters tended to be more parochial and less flexible than the opinions of those who leaned towards churches of higher denominations, in which traditionally a somewhat more worldly outlook was not considered blasphemous.

There has always been as much hypocrisy as faith in the Christian religion. Differing theologies and differing rituals still generate

The influence of the churches in helping to alleviate the poverty, malnutrition and squalor from which millions suffered was feebler than it might have been if denominational hostility had been less bitter. Dr John Clifford (*top*), leader of the Nonconformists; Dr Randall Davidson, Archbishop of Canterbury (*centre*); and Cardinal Bourne, Archbishop of Westminster (*bottom*), showed little inclination to co-operate with each other in demonstrating the realities of Christianity.

mutual mistrust between the Low Churches and the High, in spite of earnest words and pious prognostications about Church unity. The Pope remains anathema to the devout Baptist, the Salvation Army a provincial non-event to the sophisticated Jesuit. In Edwardian days, religious observance being stricter among all classes, these differences in emotional and intellectual attitudes were more conspicuous and more widely, if not more rationally, discussed. Whether they developed from the sterile arguments of opposing theologians or from a penchant for some particular clergyman, they were equally far removed from the realities of the Christian ethic. But then the Christian ethic was not something in which the Edwardians were particularly interested. The upper echelons of society were frequently amoral, self-indulgent, haughty and aimless. A little charitable work by the ladies and some display of political or professional activity by the gentlemen was seen as a sufficient justification for their way of living.

Making an appearance in Hyde Park's Rotten Row – whether to stare or be stared at – was all part of the fun of the London season.

The middle class, no less self-satisfied, was occupied chiefly with making money and with the domestic trivia of existence. The goings-on of the upper class were watched with an ambivalent gaze in which a gleam of disapproval alternated with a flicker of jealousy.

The so-called lower orders were mostly too hard worked and too busy trying to keep body and soul together for them to spend much time considering questions of ethics, Christian or otherwise. If they went to church, or more probably to chapel, it was often because they were true believers, to whom such phenomena as hell fire or the wrath of Jehovah were disturbing realities. They did not usually go, as did the fashionable world, out of a vague sense of duty – duty to the parson, to the parish, to the poor (ever in need of example) or, somewhere along the line, to God; they went to seek salvation.

For those sections of society that were better off, going to church was often little more than a dutiful preliminary to church parade, which, both in the country and in London, was as much a Sabbatical feature as the sermon or the collect. It was recognized

as a time for gossip, for picking enemies – or friends – to pieces, and for showing off the latest finery. Christian humility was usually conspicuous by its absence. In London, the stretch of Rotten Row between Marble Arch and Hyde Park Corner would be crowded with carriages in which ladies who had been worshipping at one or another of the more fashionable churches, St James's, Piccadilly, St George's, Hanover Square, or perhaps the Grosvenor Chapel in South Audley Street, displayed the latest creations of Worth, Redfern or Busvine. Behind the rails which in those days separated the road from the footpath, beings of a lesser order congregated to gape with envious enjoyment at the upper classes, to sentimentalize over their carriage horses, and to stare with suitable awe at the crested panels of their landaus or victorias.

The elegance of a carriage was still the almost universal preference of the upper crust, but here and there was soon to be seen a Rolls-Royce, a Daimler, a Mercedes-Benz, or perhaps a silent, sluggish electric brougham. Carriage traffic regulated its own speed, but in 1904 it was found necessary to impose a restriction on that of cars in the Royal parks and a limit of 10 mph was introduced, which remained in force until 1910.

The first few motor cars that appeared at church parade in Hyde Park were regarded as playthings of the very rich or the plutocratic *avant-garde*. Among the younger spectators they tended mostly to be objects of curiosity, among the older of disparagement and were generally a cause of facetious comment. Happily, both spectators and drivers were ignorant of what the motor car in course of time would be allowed to do not only to their towns and villages, but to their lives. Nor did the politicians seem particularly concerned, even though the common fallacy of equating scientific developments with scientific progress is one in which politicians, in their eagerness always to be a jump ahead of their opponents, are especially prone to express a belief. In the nine years of King Edward's reign there was an immense increase in the number of motor cars, and although the possible consequences of this were discussed at length in Parliament, little was done about the situation, for few MPs seemed to appreciate the risks inherent in the vast, rapid and uncontrolled proliferation of a device of such immense and unpredictable potentialities. To a good many other people, however, it was already apparent that there was a serious danger of the motor car becoming the public's master instead of remaining its servant.

In 1904, the first year for which reliable statistics are available, the number of cars was estimated to be 8,465. Six years later this figure had risen to 53,196 and considerable opposition was being expressed, especially in country districts, where the disturbance and inconvenience caused by cars were more directly felt than in towns and cities, whose layout, combined with the density of other traffic, tended to slow down the motorist.

In 1902, the statutory speed limit had been raised to 20 mph from the unrealistic maximum of 14 mph or less, according to the wisdom of the Local Government Board (which had in fact reduced the limit to 12 mph). The raising of this restriction on the motorist served not unnaturally to reinforce the objections of his potential victims. These objections were not simply due to a prejudice against motorists or cars as such, nor to a common suspicion of their novelty and unpredictable behaviour. As William Plowden points out in his survey of *The Motor Car and Politics*, the most obvious objection 'was the damage done to the roads, and the inconvenience caused to other road-users, by the motor car'. As cyclists had done a few years earlier, 'motorists reintroduced the idea of through traffic. Not since the great days of the stage coaches had country districts seen so much traffic merely passing through on its way to somewhere else. But the car was more dangerous than the bicycle, it did more damage to the roads . . . cars, often registered in urban districts, passed through rural areas on roads to whose upkeep their owners made no contribution, pounding them to pieces and spreading dust over crops, houses and passers-by.'

Compared with the noise, vibrations, fumes and accidents which the public has to

There's a long, long trail a-winding, and it sometimes seemed a good deal longer if you had a puncture. But the bicycle was a lot cheaper than a motor car, was easier to run, and often more reliable.

A car you could trust was what every motorist wanted, and reliability tests like the Ballinslaughter Hill climb in Ireland was watched with as much genuine interest as idle curiosity.

put up with nowadays, such objections sound almost trivial. To some Edwardians, however, they seemed substantial enough. For those who were victims of the rapidly developing craze for cars the situation was aggravated by the fact that possession of a car was still a privilege of those who, if not among the very rich, were comfortably off. As William Plowden remarks: 'It was possible to buy a car for £200 – approximately £1,200 at 1960s prices – or even less; the 5-hp Vaux-

hall, which first came out in 1903, cost £150, and the Automobile Club thought it worth organizing a Small Car Trial for cars costing under £200 as early as 1904.

'However, in the view of a motoring writer in 1904, £200 was the lowest realistic price for a touring car. . . . The car owned by the average member of the Automobile Club was more likely to cost upwards of £300. Running costs were, relative to today, even higher. Claude Johnson, the secretary of the

The motor car has long since ceased to be purely a status symbol. In the early 1900s it could hardly have been called anything else and was mostly used for such enjoyment as the primitive models of the day afforded.

Club, estimated that 10,000 miles in the lightest possible 5-horse power "voiturette" cost £67, *excluding* servicing; in a 10-hp, 2-cylinder car, £163. In a talk given to the Automobile Club at the end of 1902, one of a series pleasantly called "Motors for Men of Moderate Means", the speaker estimated his annual expenditure on a good car, costing £525, at about £335; and this excluded depreciation.

'All this must be seen against the back-ground of a society in which the average weekly wage of an adult man was less than 30 shillings, and in which only 4 per cent of the population left property worth more than £300.'

To a good many working men 30 shillings a week would have seemed a positively munificent wage. A popular sociologist, Mrs Pember Reeves, author of *Round About a Pound a Week* (1913), writing from first-hand knowledge of a number of families living in the slums of Lambeth, records that their average weekly income was only about 24 shillings a week, i.e., a little over £62 a year. The weekly expenditure in such a household would probably have been apportioned roughly as follows:

|  | s | d |
|---|---|---|
| Rent | 6 | 6 |
| Social club | | 3 |
| Funeral insurance | | 10 |
| Coal | | 9 |
| Wood and lamp oil | | 6½ |
| Soap and soda | | 10 |
| Bread (6 loaves) | 1 | 4½ |
| Meat | 3 | 2½ |
| Potatoes (8 lbs) | | 4 |
| Greens (4 lbs) | | 2 |
| Butter (½ lb) | | 6 |
| Flour (1 lb) | | 1½ |
| Dripping (½ lb) | | 3 |
| Tea (4 oz) | | 2 |
| Tin of condensed milk | | 4 |
| Husband's dinners (6d per day) | 3 | |
|  | 19s | 2d |

It will be noticed that no allowance is made for the cost of clothing or indeed any other essentials except food, heating and lighting. The amount left over, 4s 10d a week, was not much out of which to provide everything else that a family, even one living in the slums, might need for its day to day existence. But the slums, though isolated from a sizeable slice of life by poverty, were not closed communities. In London, working men and girls, especially those going to and from jobs in the West End or the City, could see plenty of evidence of an affluent society existing alongside their own indigent community, and though they might never aspire to its ranks, they could hardly help envying its members.

Such blatant disparities aroused, not unnaturally, other feelings besides envy. Throughout the whole of the Edwardian era intermittent unrest boiled and bubbled among the working classes. Though poverty was the chief cause of their discontent they were also smarting from the consequences of a situation which the law in its wisdom had recently seen fit to inflict on the working man. This was the situation precipitated by a judgement given in the High Court in what

Most slum children were permanently hungry and a two-penny eel-and-meat pie was sometimes as much as they could expect to eat in a day.

soon became an industrial *cause célèbre*, the Taff Vale case, which in its way was as important to the future of the working class community as had been the case of the Tolpuddle Martyrs in 1834.

In 1900, men employed by the Taff Vale Railway Company, a remote and obscure branch of the railway system in South Wales, came out on strike, but without the authority of their union, the Amalgamated Society of Railway Servants. In an effort to defeat the strikers, the management took on blackleg labour. This, as the management was well aware (its subsequent actions suggested that it had joyfully anticipated such a confrontation) obliged the Union to choose between a refusal to intervene and giving its members official backing. It chose the latter course. Strike pay was doled out to the workers from Union funds and efforts made to dissuade the blacklegs from working. The management retaliated by bringing an action against the Union (it being alleged that during outbreaks of violence some of the company's property had been damaged) and seeking an injunction to prevent the Union from doing anything that might harm the Company's business operations. The Company won both its cases. As a result of the first it was awarded damages of £23,000, a colossal amount by the standard of such awards at that time; in the second it was granted the injunction it had sought. Appeals by the Union were carried as far as the House of Lords, and there, in 1901, the judgements in both cases were upheld.

The effect of this decision was virtually to nullify the legal status of trade unions as it had been established by law in 1871; so in 1903, the government, recognizing the difficulties which this situation might lead to, appointed a royal commission to examine the whole question of strikes and the position of trade unions. With allowance for the complexity of both issues, the commission certainly took its time; it was not until 1906 that its report was produced. This showed a majority to be in favour of amending the law relating to picketing and conspiracy, but against any interference with the law as it had been interpreted in the Taff Vale judgement.

Once more, the government, with an eye to the changing face of the electorate, as the Labour Party increased in size and influence, soft-pedalled the issue and in the Trade Disputes Act, introduced later in the year, the commission's majority view on the inviolability of the Taff Vale judgement was thrown out. The echoes of history, reverberating down the years, have produced few sounds harsher than the growls and threats of trade union militants, who, seventy years after that foolish judgement, show that in a jaundiced few the spirit of hatred it engendered is as much alive as ever, that any and every attempt to limit the authority of trade union power in the public interest will be fought tooth and nail.

It is not in the nature of the extremist that he should ever admit satisfaction. The term extremism is relative, always leaving something more to be desired. How much more this must have meant in Edwardian days can only be dimly appreciated now through bald, impersonal statistics or glimpsed at with perhaps a little more feeling through details such as those that Mrs Pember Reeves' study provides. It is difficult to believe that things could have been worse than in the Lambeth slums, where, in the tradition of Henry Mayhew and anticipating the unscientific but painstaking methods of Mass Observation, she creates the dismal, grim, penurious picture of which some details have already been given. But in country districts things were often worse. Owing to long-standing arrangements for the importation of American wheat, agriculture had for some time been a depressed industry and when set against the drudgery of a factory or workshop, the compensations of an outdoor life and such luxuries as skimmed milk and an occasional egg didn't amount to much.

And there was doubtful gratification for the farm labourer in knowing that in spite of the depression he was still worth his hire, for that, too, didn't amount to much. At hiring fairs, which were held in various parts of the country at the beginning of the autumn, there was a possibility of getting regular work which would last throughout the

Though the labourer might be worthy of his hire, he could still be out of a job. But with luck he might find employment for the winter at a hiring fair, such as that held annually at Burford in the Cotswolds.

There were always plenty of chores to keep the children of the under-privileged busy, and in country districts none was more essential than taking Father his dinner in the fields.

winter. A 'best man' might pick up a job that would last for six months and be worth £18–20 plus board; an offer which, in default of anything else, a single man might often be tempted to accept. But of what use were such terms to a man who had a wife and family to keep?

In such circumstances the situation of a man with an income of, say, £300 a year would have seemed beyond the dreams of avarice. But the iron hand of convention kept a tighter grip on urban society than on rural communities and in town the need to maintain at least an appearance of respectability was essential in retaining the approval of one's employer and the regard of one's neighbours. On £300 life was by no means easy, even for a thrifty couple. That imperishable status symbol, a domestic servant, of however humble a grade, was regarded as an essential, even though the wife may have had no other job than to look after the house. Mrs Pember Reeves analyses the annual expenditure of such a couple living in a suburban district:

| | £ | s | d |
|---|---|---|---|
| Rent | 34 | – | – |
| Rates and taxes | 12 | – | – |
| Servant's wages | 18 | – | – |
| Washing | 26 | – | – |
| Food, for three people (and cleaning materials) | 78 | – | – |
| Wine, beer and spirits | 8 | 8 | – |
| Repairs and replacements | 10 | – | – |
| Coal and gas | 20 | – | – |
| | £206 | 8 | – |

This, as Mrs Pember Reeves points out, leaves only £93.12 'for all other expenses – doctor, chemist, dentist, charity, amusements, insurance, travelling, savings, books, papers, stamps, stationery, dress, etc.' It doesn't sound much and illness or a temporary disability could easily make things worse. Yet a couple scraping along in this way could hardly be classed as living in poverty, as were the many who lived in the slums. Researches by the pioneer sociologists Charles Booth and Seebohm Rowntree, acting separately and independently, showed how grim was the state of affairs in London and in York.

Booth and Rowntree were both rich men. Booth was a shipowner and Rowntree a cocoa manufacturer and in both of them had been inculcated the non-conformist conscience that had given so sharp a stimulus to Victorian philanthropy. It was not, however, by direct forms of charity that they aimed to relieve the situation, but by trying to discover the underlying causes of urban poverty through statistical research. We are nowadays so accustomed to the manifold uses of the dismal science that a statistical enquiry seems the most obvious basis on which to formulate plans for social change. But in adopting this method of finding out what they wanted to know, Booth and Rowntree, each in their own ways, made original and highly important contributions to sociological research.

As a young man Booth had been a radical, but as often happens, prosperity caused him to change his views. His business thrived and eventually his views became more Conservative, but he never lost interest in the living conditions of the working class. Rowntree, a Quaker, was profoundly influenced by Booth's findings and decided to try and find out if things were as bad in York, where his factory was, as in London.

Booth's survey, *Life and Labour of the People in London*, was the more massive of the two; it appeared intermittently between 1889 and 1903 and was in seventeen volumes. Rowntree's *Poverty, a Study of Town Life*, was published in 1901. It was a remarkable achievement for a young man of only thirty, for besides coping with the immense amount of work involved, Rowntree was also preoccupied with the responsibilities of a business career. *Poverty*, although based on a population of only about 75,000, revealed a picture no less disturbing than Booth had painted of conditions in London. 'We are faced,' Rowntree concluded, 'by the startling probability that from 25 to 30 per cent of the town populations of the United Kingdom are living in poverty', and by poverty he meant in actual want and slum conditions. Commenting on Rowntree's conclusions,

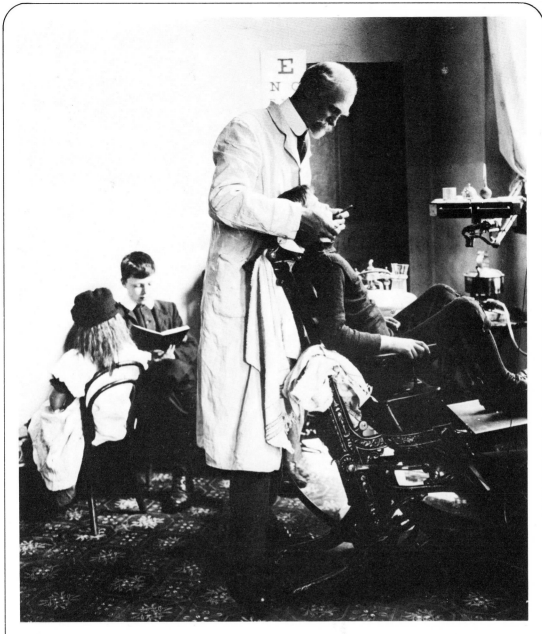

Following the publication of Seebohm Rowntree's survey, *Poverty*, in 1901, public anxiety about the effects of under-nourishment and bad housing on the working population led to the setting up of children's clinics in working-class neighbourhoods.

Donald Reed in his book *Edwardian England* points out that 'He also showed that this poverty problem was closely linked to the urban housing question and to the problem of the health of the people. Because of poverty, 6·4 per cent of the inhabitants of York lived more than two to a room, while the number who lived, and slept, in rooms which provided inadequate air space was very much greater. Rowntree noted the low physical quality of intending army recruits in York, Leeds and Sheffield; between 1897 and 1901 nearly one half were rejected on medical grounds.'

At first sight it may seem exaggerated to claim that, as a result, 'urban life was thus creating a direct threat to future national and imperial security', but throughout the Edwardian era, the tinkling music of Daly's and the Gaiety Theatres, typifying its more frivolous aspects, was counter pointed by sounds unmistakably German, which produced at first a faint, and then by degrees a more bellicose accompaniment. Although by 1914 there may have been some improvement in the standard of physical fitness, it might well have seemed to the Kaiser, encouraged by Rowntree's disclosures, that in the event of war Britain's 'contemptible little army', as he later called it, would not be able to offer much resistance to the German war machine.

Both the public and the government were startled by the facts disclosed by Rowntree's survey, and considerably dismayed when their effects on army recruiting were confirmed by the director-general of the Army Medical Service. The government was sufficiently perturbed to appoint a committee 'To determine, with the aid of such counsel as the medical profession are able to give, the steps that should be taken to furnish the Government and the Nation at large with periodical data for an accurate estimate of the health and physique of the people.'

The Committee's enquiries, while serving to moderate the worst prognostications about recruiting, dredged up a considerable amount of discreditable though nonetheless valuable evidence about rotten housing, bad sanitation, air pollution, venereal disease and other factors affecting the lives of the poor. The Committee's report was in a sense the starting point of a movement towards social reform which eventually involved substantial improvements in public health, education, working conditions and care for the unemployed and the destitute.

Rowntree had calculated that in a town the lowest sum on which a man with a wife and three children could live was 21s 8d a week, or about £55 a year. This of course, allowed only for the basic necessities of existence; even small luxuries were out of the question. Not everyone would have agreed on what constituted a luxury. The absolute indispensability of a retinue of servants, not to mention a carriage and pair, would no doubt have been powerfully argued by those who had been accustomed to such things all their lives.

One of the penalties of being rich, especially through inheritance – self-made millionaires have usually had experience of other and inferior life styles – is that it tends to diminish the sense of proportion, to make that which is merely convenient seem imperative. The tenacity with which this easy illusion is sometimes clung to intensifies the mutual suspicion that must always exist between the haves and the have-nots. The Goncourts remarked that 'there are two great currents in human history: baseness, which makes conservatives; and envy, which makes revolutionaries'. It is a simplification of the kind the Goncourts were prone to make, based on their own somewhat limited observations, but it is a simplification that is not without some truth. Along with their 'two great currents' flows the class consciousness that for many generations has provided English politics, literature and conversation with an apparently inexhaustible theme. And at no period in British history has society as a whole been more class conscious than it was in Edwardian days. During the preceding era, as is shown in the novels of writers like Dickens, Trollope and Thackeray, with allowance for their exaggerations of character and feeling, consciousness of class divisions certainly existed, but were accepted on the whole as part of the natural order of things. The novels of the period do not harp continually on the subject, nor do their characters show themselves to be anxiously preoccupied by it, as were the Edwardians. But there were reasons for their preoccupation.

Compared with the intermittent bouts of democratic fever that had earlier broken out in Europe, Chartism, an infection confined to Britain and which had first been observed in 1838, had seemed like a mild rash and by 1850 it had been eradicated. It took some fifty years for echoes of the ominous rumblings of 1848 to reach Britain from the

Continent. Not for the first or last time, the country's geographical isolation from the rest of Europe turned out to be of profound importance to its destiny, for it is difficult to believe that if in 1848 the British Isles had been part of the mainland of Europe the momentous events of that year would not have had a significant effect on public feeling and political policy.

In 1870, Dickens, in an audience with Queen Victoria, had affirmed his belief that 'the division of classes in England ... would get better in time'. He felt sure that it would come gradually. Within three months of their conversation Dickens was dead. The Queen, commenting on his death in her journal, showed that she had not forgotten his remarks: 'He felt sure that a better feeling, and much greater union of classes would take place in time. And,' she added significantly, 'I pray earnestly it may'.

Such sentiments are not readily associated with Queen Victoria, but in fact she was being perfectly sincere. She may sometimes have been prejudiced, sometimes obstinate, often illogical, and may not always have practised what she preached, but she had neither the will nor the wit to play the part of a cynic. She was certainly no fool either, and well understood that the immediate causes of class divisions were not inherent in human nature, but arose because of the imperfections of human institutions and were therefore susceptible of adjustment. But that adjustment, as Dickens had emphasised, must be gradual. The reason that the Queen disliked and feared radicalism was that its proponents in their inevitable impatience seemed to represent the forces of darkness, violence and coercion.

King Edward was not as shrewd by nature as his 'dear Mama' and lacked her instinct in political matters, as well as her experience of them, though this was not through any fault of his own but rather through her treatment of him. He did not by any means regard democracy as inevitable, however gradual its achievement. He 'was eager to see suffering relieved, but', as Philip Magnus has pointed out, 'he equated socialist remedies with revolution. He feared the risk of damage to the organic structure of a hierarchical society which he regarded as divinely ordained. . . .'

This view of the divine will, the operation of which was presumably thought to be suspended during the more frolicsome interludes of the King's association with Lady Warwick, Lillie Langtry, Mrs James Hartmann, Alice Keppel or Agnes Keyser, stopped short of the distasteful notion that all men are equal in the sight of God. Only revolutionaries or religious maniacs could seriously entertain such a belief and indeed very few people did. But 1848, and more recently the Reform Bill of 1884, had given the upper and middle classes a jolt. People were getting ideas above their station. One had only to look about one to see how serious was the threat to the order and stability of society.

This alarming situation was observable in every sphere, but in none was it more apparent than in domestic service, that great preoccupation of the Edwardian middle class. And since it loomed so large in their lives it may be worth taking a closer look at the situation. Domestic service covers a variety of different and not always neatly categorized types of employment, but such figures as there are indicate that in the years 1905 to 1910, certainly no less than 2 million people, the vast majority of whom were women, were engaged in some form of domestic service.

To all but the very rich, practically all that remains of that once indispensable and onerous calling are the 'daily', the au pair, and that all-purpose unit, the 'foreign couple', usually seeking a respite from the harsh realities of poverty or unemployment in Italy, Spain or Portugal. The luxury of a full domestic staff is often thought of nowadays not merely as a hedonistic indulgence, but as an affront to the dignity of man. That in the old days some servants may actually have enjoyed their work, may have taken a pride in doing it well and felt no sense of degradation in their menial status, is likely to be dismissed as irrelevant by a generation nourished on the doctrine that the only acceptable and worthwhile form of service is that which is given to the community as a

*Left :* The Countess of Warwick, with her son Maynard. The Countess was one of several ladies who helped King Edward to prolong into old age the reputation of being a gay Lothario.

It is estimated that throughout the Edwardian era about two million of the working-class population were in domestic service. Most were women and a staff of four would not have been unusual for a middle-class family of the same number.

whole and that there is something reprehensible about a relationship that involves payment of one individual for domestic services received by another. Those without experience of such a relationship often find it hard to imagine that a strong bond of mutual loyalty and liking could ever have existed between the master or the mistress of a household and his or her servants. The situation is liable to be thought of as one that must inevitably have involved lofty condescension on the one hand and enforced subservience on the other.

Perhaps in some cases, though it seems unlikely that they were ever in the majority, there may be some degree of truth in this generalization. Some mistresses may have treated their servants like dirt, but a more common form of exploitation and oppression was likely to have been the exercise of authority by higher servants, usually butlers and cooks, over those lower down in the strict hierarchy of the servants' hall. Officious bullying of this sort or the unkindness or lack of consideration of a stupid mistress may have contributed to the unpopularity of domestic service, both among girls and men, which began to be noticeable in Edwardian days. But it was with the First World War that the disintegration of domestic service as part of the social structure really started, though not until the Second was it virtually completed.

Ideas above their station was often a convenient imputation to attach to servants who left their jobs because of intolerable working conditions. Mrs Dorothy Peel, an author of several popular books about household management and domestic economy, showed a more realistic understanding of the aspirations of over-worked and under-paid junior maids. In *How to Keep House* (1902), she refers to some of the difficulties in the way of getting servants: '. . . an important fault is that mistresses fail to move with the times, and to realize that the ideas and requirements of the working classes have altered considerably during the last few years, and that servants require higher wages and more liberty than they have hitherto expected.

'The young working-girl of today prefers to become a Board School mistress, a post-office clerk, a typewriter, a shop girl or a worker in a factory – anything rather than domestic service; not because the work is lighter or the pay better, but because in these professions she has the full use of her hours of liberty, and, more important reason than all, she enjoys a higher social position: she is in fact a "young lady".'

Since the size of an Edwardian staff was considered a pointer to the social status of its employer, it followed that an enormous number of men and women of all ages were

In order to ensure a continuous supply of servants there were schools that specialised in teaching young girls the various skills and duties of domestic service.

engaged in domestic service, which ranged, among indoor servants, from the butler to the scullery maid, or, if a page was kept, to the 'buttons'. Their responsibilities and skills varied from duties involving a high degree of trust or expertise, such as a sound knowledge of wines or cigars, to tasks whose drudgery and boredom made them fit only for young people of sub-normal intelligence. There is a touch of black comedy about an Edwardian story concerning one such girl, eventually driven mad by the cruel monotony of her job, who, in the asylum where she was sent, refused to make the beds, complaining that as soon as she had made them someone slept in them again. Her situation was probably not very different from that in which a good many maids-of-all-work found themselves, involving a self-perpetuating routine of washing, cleaning or preparing something so that someone else might be able to dirty it or use

it later on, in order that she should wash it, clean it, or prepare it once again.

Mrs Peel, in *How to Keep House*, differentiates between some twenty-five types of indoor servant, each of whose sphere of activities was often as rigidly laid down as that of any shop-floor worker in a modern factory. Cook, the acknowledged suzeraine of the female staff, might, if she were that type of gorgon, deal with any infringement of the rules as severely and maliciously as a bloody-minded shop steward will sometimes deal with the minor transgressions of his fellow workers. Mrs Peel's summaries of servants' duties show not only how precise was their allocation, but how laborious were some of the jobs that had to be done. Under the heading of Arrangement of Work in a Small Town House (2 servants and a nurse), she sets out the following house-parlourmaid's timetable:

Down 6.30; do drawing-room and morning-room (gas fire in latter); get breakfast for 8 [a.m.]; have own breakfast; go up to bedrooms, do bedroom work and cleaning till 11.30; wash breakfast things and do knives; dress; lay and serve lunch; see to fires; have own dinner; clear lunch and wash up; do pantrywork, needlework; answer door-bell; take tea; shut up sitting rooms; ring dressing gong; set table; see to fires and tidy up drawing-room; serve dinner; clear, wash up; bed at 10.

In addition to all this, special chores were allotted to each day, except Sunday. However, there is an understandable evasiveness in Mrs Peel's time-table about the precise hours at which these chores were to be slotted into the daily routine; it might well seem that the house-parlourmaid would already have had enough on her hands without having to give a thought to—

*Monday.* – Morning left free for silver and pantry work; afternoon, do linen for wash.

*Tuesday.* – Morning, turn out best bedroom; afternoon, needlework.

*Wednesday.* – Morning, turn out master's room and bathroom; afternoon, mending.

*Thursday.* – Morning, turn out servants' rooms; afternoon, mending.

*Friday.* – Morning, pantry cleaning and silver; afternoon, for own needlework.

*Saturday.* – Morning, stairs and lavatories; afternoon, do linen and put out fresh towels, etc.

And what sort of wages would this industrious paragon have received? The cynical resignation of Mrs Peel's smile can be imagined as she makes a comparison between the wage rates recommended by Mrs Beeton in the first edition of *Household Management*, published in 1859, and those that she herself found to represent a reasonable average in 1902, 'after inquiry at registry offices and perusal of advertisements'.

The house-parlourmaid was a hybrid unknown to Mrs Beeton, but would presumably have found her place, if she had existed then, between the upper-housemaid, paid at the rate of £12–£20 per year, and the maid-of-all-work, who got £9–£14. Already in 1902 the greedy spectre of inflation was licking its

goblin chops and a head housemaid, the equivalent of Mrs Beeton's upper-housemaid, could command £24–£30 a year and a between-maid £10–£18. A professed cook – that is, one who had no other job than to prepare the meals – could pull down as much as £30–£60 a year, and a cook-housekeeper, who combined supervision of the staff with her job in the kitchen, £30–£80.

Rules of dress for domestic servants were almost as strict as Queen's Regulations on the subject of military uniforms – and this in spite of the fact that both housemaids and parlourmaids, unlike the subterranean cook, were expected to provide their own 'print and black gowns, caps and aprons'. If something more elaborate in the way of dress or of livery for menservants was required the mistress would provide it, as for instance a powdered wig, although, says Mrs Peel, 'only those who have considerable households expect their footmen to wear powder'. Menservants were 'always expected to be clean shaved, except in the case of a soldier servant, who wears a moustache'.

This dispensation stemmed perhaps from the difficulty of always presenting a clean-shaved face on the field of battle and perhaps served as a reminder to the other servants that the military man, by virtue of his experience overseas or attendance in the officers' mess, was a cut above the rest of them, always excepting of course the butler, that autocrat of the breakfast, luncheon and dinner table (the tea table being of course the prerogative of the upper housemaid).

Among a staff large enough to include a butler, the allocation of their duties as between one type of servant and another would be almost as strict as their rules of dress and most of their tasks would be performed without the benefit of labour-saving devices. Such devices as did exist were often crude and unreliable, and there were few solvents or detergents of the kind in use today. Nor were there any of those incidental aids such as transistor radios or television, without which the labours of Sisyphus would seem preferable to the lot of the modern *au pair*. It was by human energy alone that those unending household chores were got through that are today done by electricity, and will no doubt be done in the not too distant future by atomic power. Until that Elysium is reached, however, we shall not know whether the atom will be more efficient than the dogged domestic; whether glass will gleam as brightly as it used to on Edwardian dinner tables; whether rugs and carpets will be brushed and rooms dusted as thoroughly; paintwork cleaned as spotlessly; beds made as quickly and neatly; and as much care be given to keeping clean the synthetic bric-a-brac of the modern open-plan living room as when Mrs Peel's between-maid slogged through her daily routine for a reward of £10 to £18 a year.

Not only were Edwardian servants dependent on their own efforts to fulfil the demands of house-proud and exacting mistresses, their tasks were often complicated by the dictates of popular taste. Although houses differed in design, they continued to be built and rooms to be furnished no less elaborately than in the mid-Victorian seventies. The arty influence of William Morris on designers neither as sensitive nor as discreet as himself had its result in fussy and self-conscious effects that were quite the opposite of his own earthy aims. Fireplaces were adorned with extravagantly ornamental

*Art nouveau et l'art bourgeois.* Modern ideas about furnishing and decoration, as revealed (*above*) at the Glasgow Exhibition of Decorative and Industrial Art in 1901, made slow headway at first, but gradually began to affect the long-lasting legacy of Victorian taste (*opposite*), with its clash of styles and clutter of ornaments.

but useless canopies, usually of white-painted wood or stained oak and sometimes incorporating a range of open shelves for the display of Moorish or Germanic faience, both of which were popular. De Morgan tiles, for some time the hallmark of *avant-garde* taste, or others in the same dull colours, were also much in vogue. Furniture designers, harking back to the emasculated forms of Hepplewhite, himself arguably a less original and less self-assured *ébéniste* than either Chippendale or Sheraton, produced a type of spindly, attenuated furniture that was both undistinguished and uncomfortable. Much of it was fragile to look at and often upholstered in dim anaemic colours; or else the style was debased in a way that foreshadowed the bogus Tudor vogue that was to make a mockery of the good intentions of garden city fathers in such new suburbs as Welwyn or Golders Green.

There was also a taste for ornamental plaques or vessels of indeterminate use made of beaten copper or pewter, which was sometimes decorated with abstract blobs of bright vitreous enamel. Tortuous table lamps of the same metals or of brass were adorned with pleated silk shades decked with bows and flounces. Parquet floors strewn with oriental or fur rugs were found preferable to carpets, a change perhaps for the better, since those of English manufacture were usually of surpassing ugliness. The cult of simplicity on which all this was based had become a myth. Under the half-digested Continental influence of *art nouveau* domestic design went berserk, but with results that were often not so much outrageous as pathetic.

The ugliness of much domestic design was the product of sterility, not over-exuberance, such as had resulted in some of the clumsy and elaborate furnishing fantasies of the Crystal Palace period. Much that was shown at the Great Exhibition in 1851 was attractive and ingenious; but there was also much that was hideous, complicated and useless. There were pianos that looked like monstrous pieces of confectionery; there were bee-hives disguised as chests of drawers; there were fire-irons that might have served as well for the weapons of a crusader; there was even a garden seat made of coal and a curious candelabrum with a base in the shape of two recumbent camels.

Perhaps it was partly as reaction against the legacy of all this, which continued to manifest itself in various forms until about the turn of the century, that the Edwardian domestic arts took on such a chapped and chilled appearance. But such a reaction would account for only part of the pitiful decline in the arts by which the Edwardian era was afflicted. Their vitality was sapped by a more deep-seated malaise.

It is impossible for any of the arts to flourish in an atmosphere of indifference. Intelligent criticism and discussion are as necessary to artists as total self-sufficiency is rare among them. In Edwardian England the arts had a pretty thin time. King Edward knew nothing and cared less about painting, literature or music. He could probably not have named as many as a dozen artists, alive or dead, he was impatient of all but martial music, and he was bored by books. In a letter to Mr Gladstone in 1872 (Edward was then over thirty), Queen Victoria explained that 'the P. of W. has *never* been fond of reading, and that from his earliest years it was *impossible* to get him to do so. Newspapers and, *very rarely*, a novel, are all he ever reads.'

His example was not encouraging to those who comprised the Court circle. High society can only retain its elevated position by taking its cue from the sovereign or ruler and the circles in which King Edward moved were as indifferent to the arts as he was. The meagre encouragement they received probably reflected public taste fairly accurately and it is hardly surprising that the first decade of the twentieth century was one of the most depressing that the arts in Britain have ever passed through. The timidity, the silliness, and the pomposity of much that was written or produced make a poor showing by comparison with what was happening abroad. For a variety of historical reasons, the British have never excelled either in painting or in music, though in architecture, as in writing, they have produced a few men of genius comparable with the great architects of Italy, France and Germany. But that was before King Edward's reign and their successors during that period were usually outstanding only for the banality of their conceptions. That so much Edwardian municipal architecture escaped the blitz is one of the misfortunes of war. That which was spared often combines a marked unsuitability for its purpose with a flamboyance that seems to derive from ill-observed Classical and Baroque forms. From a herd of prosaic architects working on these lines a few stand out as being less intimidated by tradition than the rest and somewhat less afraid of exercising their imaginations. Domestic architecture in particular was influenced by a handful of men such as Norman Shaw, Sir Edwin Lutyens, Rennie Mackintosh and C.A.Voysey, but even their conceptions often show traces of that arty-craftiness that laid its damp hand on so many British products and designs of the period. In architecture, as in other manifestations of the spirit of an age, that age usually gets what it deserves and if the Edwardians got stuck with the various pretentious pseudo-styles that characterize the period, this must surely be because they expressed no desire for anything more interesting or more adventurous.

Although in literature, seen in the un-

Literary lions. Among a galaxy of famous and popular authors, most of them now all but forgotten, as are their works, were Elinor Glyn (*top left*), Anthony Hope (*top right*), Marie Corelli (*centre*), Hall Caine (*bottom left*), and Charles Garvice (*bottom right*).

compromising glare of hindsight, things appear rather better, it could hardly be said that King Edward's reign was a golden age. Nor can this be accounted for simply by the fact that he reigned for a comparatively short time. It is one of the ironies of being a modern celebrity that fame seldom lasts beyond the gates of the crematorium. The names of innumerable novelists, poets, dramatists, critics and journalists who were favourites of the Edwardian reading public are now not only forgotten by those who read their works at the time, but to a whole generation are completely unknown. How many reputations once so large and luminous, so widely respected, have sunk without trace? And sunk in little more than half a lifetime. Hall Caine, Marie Corelli, Charles Garvice, Elinor Glyn, Nat Gould, Robert Hitchens, Anthony Hope, Leonard Merrick, Rita,

Temple Thurston, W.B.Maxwell – all of them in their day were widely read and enthusiastically discussed, though none of them had the means of publicizing their works or boosting their reputations that most modern authors can rely on. There was no television or radio; films were still a form of primitive entertainment; paperbacks of the modern sort were unknown; and serial possibilities were negligible compared with those that today's newspapers or magazines have to offer.

The natural process by which mediocrity is weeded out and trash eliminated repeats itself in every generation. Most of today's favourites are heading, poor things, for tomorrow's oblivion – most, though not all. Yet who shall say which of them already emits the sweet scent of immortality? The peculiar alchemy of public taste has ensured the survival of a handful of Edwardian authors. Thomas Hardy, Henry James (both Edwardians only by a narrow margin), Shaw, Wells, Bennett, Galsworthy and Maugham seem to have done rather better than, for example, Kipling, Barrie, Rider Haggard and Chesterton. This is not the place to examine the complex probabilities that might explain the survival of some or the swift eclipse of others. The fact remains that each of them in their various ways struck up a satisfactory and successful relationship with the Edwardian public.

Were the Edwardians, then, less critical, more easily satisfied by mediocrity than are we, the neo-Elizabethans? It would hardly seem so, judging from some trends in modern writing. The Edwardians' code of manners was appropriate to their own times and in many ways would seem absurdly stuffy nowadays, but their circumlocutions and reticence in dealing with sex, for instance, were perhaps not as foolish as some of their other restrictive practices. It can hardly be supposed that the common use of four-letter words would have added anything worthwhile to the Edwardian novel, the limitations of which may now seem rather artificial. But however hypocritical Edwardian society may have been, its appreciation of self-restraint, the basis of good manners, its ability to keep a stiff upper lip, and its mistrust of sensationalism were perfectly genuine. Such considerations, however, are hardly enough on which to establish a significant output of writing, and that the literature of the period was saved from the debilitating effects of a surfeit of romance and good breeding was due to authors like Shaw, Yeats, Chesterton, Wells, the egregious Harris, Bennett and others who were concerned not with jejune fantasies acted out in Ruritania or on the shores of some blue lagoon, but with the complexities of the human condition.

With painting it was a different matter. A handful of solitary geniuses who have little in common, Hilliard, Hogarth, Wilson, Stubbs, Turner, and perhaps one or two more, do not by themselves constitute a tradition such as is sustained in English literature by a long and continuous succession of inspired writers. English art has never been more than a poor relation of the great schools of the Continent. In the Edwardian era it became practically destitute. The rot had set in with the unctuous art of the late Victorians, though the Victorian period as a whole had been one of lively enterprise. Its diversity of attitudes and skills ranged from the Pre-Raphaelites' to Whistler's and from Samuel Palmer's to Alma Tadema's. At the beginning of the century, of those painters of distinction who had resisted the Royal Academy's suffocating embrace, few were still alive. By 1903, the foremost of these, Whistler, was dead, leaving only Sickert and a handful of others to maintain the proposition that art was concerned with more interesting and complex questions than how to decorate a biscuit box or paint a pretty calendar. The Edwardians, having on the whole no higher expectations of its possibilities, were easily diverted by anything that looked like a novelty, such as the problem pictures of the Honourable John Collier, whose chief mystery consisted in the reason for their popularity, except as gimmicks for those who are easily beguiled by such things.

The general run of Edwardian art was deplorable and the intellectual lethargy of

Danger – Marcus Stone at work. The scenes of Regency coquettishness in which Stone excelled, and repeated *ad nauseam*, pandered to a sloppy and unenterprising public whose only requirement of art was that its appreciation should need no effort.

the middle class a godsend to many a competent hack who had established himself in a profitable niche. The Royal Academy was regarded as the shrine of art and throughout the period its high priest and president was Sir Edward Poynter, whose stale concepts, closely following the style and idiom of his mentor, Lord Leighton, himself not a great artist, were characterized by a self-conscious grandeur that only emphasised their inadequacy.

But Poynter was only one of many who cashed in on the public's sentimental apathy. Joseph Farquharson's endless repetitions of sheep in snowy landscapes and the languid Regency flirtations of Marcus Stone made no demands of any sort on one's critical faculties. Nor did the sloppy chivalric visions of Frank Dicksee, Briton Rivière's tedious studies of the brute creation, varied now and then by a touch of roguish sentiment, or the sickening, saintly innocents portrayed by James Sant, as in that popular nursery picture, *The Soul's Awakening*.

John Singer Sargent, the Anglo-American portrait painter, whose acute perception of both the best and the worst characteristics of Edwardian high society made him in his day the most famous artist in Britain.

example, by the Camden Town Group – Sickert, Gilman, Gore among others – to be brought to the surface. Its members made no concessions to popular taste and espoused revolutionary ideas about art. Sargent's art was conservative and his worldly success may well have made him suspect to the *avant-garde*, but until the sporadic appearances of Graham Sutherland as a portrait painter some fifty years later, Sargent remained supreme in the twentieth century. However critical or influential his sitters were, he was never afraid to paint them, warts and all. Yet such was the power of his reputation and such the conceit of society that its members suffered themselves willingly to be crucified on his easel.

Sargent's achievement, however, was not simply aesthetic. No contemporary memoirs, no published letters, reported speeches or journalistic profiles reveal more dispassionately the essential character of that minute though disproportionately influential section of society, the British aristocracy. And on the whole the picture was not an edifying one. 'The whole of society,' as Anita Leslie observes in her account of its love affairs, '... constituted an entity with mutual interests', namely, those of ensuring the right marriages and inheritances and the preservation of property and privilege. The constant traits of its members were an unassailable self-satisfaction and a steely snobbishness. Intelligence, grace, wit and vivacity may be there too, but they cannot disguise the innate sense of God-given superiority, the certainty that power of place is the aristocracy's natural preserve and patronage an act of self-sacrifice rather than of condescension. These sincerely-held but disagreeable illusions Sargent exposed to view with perfect candour, but without cynicism, and mysteriously the public fell for his portraits as readily as for Dicksee's anaemic damozels and Marcus Stone's mawkish scenes of dalliance.

It was not only painting, however, that suffered through the public's preference for the literal, the coy, and the cosy; music shared the same sort of fate. The attitude of the majority was aptly summarized by Sir

That artists of such indifferent skill and weak imagination as Collier, Dicksee or Farquharson could make the grade did not preclude an accidental preference for something better, if occasionally something better turned up. It has become fashionable to decry the work of John Singer Sargent as being repetitive and sometimes showy in its technique, and there is some justification for both these criticisms. But Sargent's deadpan scrutiny of the upper crust of Edwardian society is often as telling in its uncompromising penetration as the portraiture of Hals or Van Dyck. Not that Sargent even in his own time was without his critics. Yet those who claimed that there were other artists quite as talented and often more interesting than Sargent found it hard to make their voices heard. In a decade as stagnant in all the arts it was difficult for unconventional talents, such as those represented, for

Osbert Sitwell: '... in music the English know what they like, jolly bumpy tunes, of a short line of melody, and with the bleat of a Southdown sheep never far from their core'.

Such stuff appealed particularly to Edwardian ears, in which the commonplace musical sounds of Victorian times still reverberated. Music, in fact, had been bottom of the class in Britain since the days of Purcell. The short-lived period in which the collective genius of the English lutanists, Dowland, Campion, Ford and a few others, flowered and flourished was unique. Since that time, although Germany, Italy and France had each produced a succession of composers whose fame was world-wide, all that Britain had had to offer were the burblings of composers like Arne, Balfe, Sullivan and Stanford. To this not very inspiring galaxy there was one exception – Sir Edward Elgar. Although he was a mid-Victorian by birth, Elgar did not really catch the public ear until the turn of the century and by then he was demonstrably so far in advance of any other British composer that even the public could not fail to realize it. What distinguished him from the others was his ability not only to write music that appealed to popular taste, music that was sometimes sentimental, sometimes bombastic, and always and inescapably English, but also music to which knowledgeable critics paid serious attention.

Probably the most significant influence on musical taste during the Edwardian period was not, however, that of a composer, but of a conductor, Sir Henry Wood, at whose Promenade Concerts at the Queen's Hall

The Queen's Hall (now demolished), though an architectural monstrosity, was significant musically as the scene of Sir Henry Wood's Promenade Concerts. These were influential in stimulating a genuine musical interest among the general public.

many thousands of listeners were given for the first time, and at prices they could afford, opportunities to hear the great musical classics played by a fine orchestra. Sir Henry's programmes may not seem particularly enterprising by modern standards, but undoubtedly they were of enormous importance in stimulating public interest.

Since the advent of radio the British public's appreciation of music has undergone a transformation that few Edwardians would have believed remotely possible, had some omniscient critic been able to predict it. In art, too, though for reasons more complex than the change in musical taste, a new awareness and curiosity have been aroused. The derision that at first greeted the work of artists such as Picasso, Modigliani, Klee or Léger has turned to sincere and widespread admiration. Indeed, the pendulum has not simply swung forward; in some cases it has left its pivot, so that any old rubbish painted or assembled in the name of art will find some

eager admirers to chase after it with one arm outstretched and the other clinging to the bandwagon of the *avant-garde*. In writing, too, works that would have puzzled or angered most Edwardians by writers such as Huxley, Joyce, Beckett or Auden, are widely recognized as contributions of permanent importance to English literature.

If the British attitude towards the arts has undergone a significant change since Edwardian days, the attitude to sport has changed no less. From being looked upon simply as an agreeable means of recreation, sport has become a national fetish with highly organized and complex rites involving the collection of vast sums of tribute.

Man for man, the British are probably more addicted to sport than any other nation. Whatever the reason, whether it lies in our island status, our climate, geography, nutritional habits, or some other basic circumstances, as a nation we have always found in sport a satisfaction unsurpassed by almost

The British passion for sport has always gone hand in hand with a passion for gambling, for which the Derby was a golden opportunity. There was betting, too, on the Cup Final, to which thousands of spectators went in procession.

any other activity. It is not too fanciful to imagine that our primeval ancestors hunting the elk or the mammoth for food enjoyed doing so as much for the excitement of the chase as for its rewards. Eating, idling, disputation and other easeful pursuits have never had the same attractions for us as they have for the peoples of the Continent. In Britain, the throwing, hitting or kicking of a ball have always seemed more worthwhile ways of passing the time.

Although in Edwardian days sport was already becoming something of a national preoccupation, a sense of proportion was still preserved about its relative importance in the scheme of things. It was regarded primarily as a means of recreation, not as the livelihood of promoters, managers, bookmakers, tipsters, commentators and other peripheral figures who have helped to turn sport into big business. Yet even in Edwardian days the entrepreneur and the middle-

man were already on the make, for there were rich pickings to be had from exploiting the sporting public. The Cup Final, then held at the Crystal Palace, attracted up to 100,000 spectators and at weekends large crowds attended sporting functions of all sorts up and down the country.

The appeal of sport varied, as it does now, from class to class and from one generation to another. Soccer, which was considered decidedly plebeian, today has its devotees in every class. Racing was the only sport whose appeal may be said to have been truly universal, as it still is. King Edward's enthusiasm for the Turf and his constant attendance at race meetings ensured that there would be a fashionable crowd wherever he went, and the Englishman's consuming passion for gambling also drew to the race course both the middle and working classes.

The Edwardians, without making a fetish of sport, found plenty of ways of exercising and enjoying themselves simultaneously. Cricket, tennis, golf, hockey, croquet, athletics, archery and cycling were among their outdoor pastimes, though these were

With ball and mallet in deepest Woking.
Croquet was one of the few sports that women
could enjoy without fear of being condemned
as unladylike.

mostly the prerogative of the middle class,
as hunting, shooting and fishing (which
meant by definition fishing for salmon or
trout; roach, chub or other such unmention-
able creatures were strictly for the lower
orders) were the preserve of the rich. It was
therefore as onlookers more often than as
participants that the poor enjoyed sports,
though their vicarious pleasure as spectators
was probably as genuine as that of supporters
who crowd the stands at Highbury or the
Oval today. Apart from the expense, however, the poor would have suffered from a
handicap no less formidable had they at-
tempted to encroach on the pastimes of their
betters. Prejudice is seldom susceptible to

reason, especially the type of prejudice that
gave rise in cricket to the distinction that
gentlemen chose to draw between themselves and players.

The mystique of cricket, except the village
variety, was comprehended in its highest
form only by the upper and middle classes,
to whom the simile of the straight bat exem-
plified the correct way of playing not only
against the opposing team, but also the larger
game of life. Lords Cricket Ground still had
a place in the sun. The Eton and Harrow
match was a devotional exercise of the London season which it would have been as
unthinkable to neglect as a summons to
Buckingham Palace. County champion-
ships, though of a lower order in the eyes of
Society, attracted congregations even more
devout, for it was the play that counted on
such occasions, not the glory of one's

Any more for the Skylark? Passing through Boulter's Lock *en route* for the Golden Mile at Henley Royal Regatta.

apparel or the strawberries and cream. The Anglo-Indian colonel in his blazer and panama hat, seated silent and attentive in the Members' Stand, epitomized the order and tranquillity that characterize the sacred rites of the game.

Henley Royal Regatta was another important fixture in the sporting calendar and as a Society event was hardly less significant than the Eton and Harrow match. To be seen, or to watch others, languid in a punt at Boulter's Lock or strolling about in the Members' enclosure was as necessary a part of the proceedings as the race for the Grand Challenge Cup.

Professionalism in sport may have diminished the pulling power and prowess of the amateur; it may have increased the excitement of the onlooker; and it has certainly enriched a multitude for whom the money involved is what matters most. To the Edwardians, a sport was still a game; it could never have been envisaged by a gentleman, and probably not even by a player, as the source of a super-taxed income or a substitute for religion. It carried with it neither the anxieties or responsibilities associated with the one, nor the artificial sense of values and emotional wear and tear of the latter.

Like the rest of life, sport has undergone immense changes and innovations since the Edwardian decade, but few of those changes or innovations suggest that it has become more enjoyable for the sportsman than when Kipling's flannelled fool, the true Edwardian amateur, played the game of his choice for no better reason than that he loved it.

In retrospect the Edwardians seem in many ways not very different from the late Victorians. Although they may have seen themselves as the gleaming heralds of a new age – an understandable illusion after so long a period spent in submission to the stolid attitudes and rigid conventions of the previous era–they were not really very different from their immediate predecessors. In their political ideals, their moral beliefs and social theories, their scientific thinking, their educational concepts, their arts and their manners, they were considerably closer to the Victorian era than to the strenuous, cynical, emancipated world that was rapidly to succeed their own. The Great War was also the Great Divide: the twentieth century started late, not in 1900, but in 1919, and by that time King Edward had been dead for more than nine years.

It was said of Gladstone, and often repeated about Asquith, the provincial nonconformist who made the grade by obliterating an unpropitious background with the help of a rich and pushing wife – it was said of him that although he was in Society, he was never of it; one of those characteristically snobbish assertions of the kind the Edwardians were prone to make about each other. Of themselves it might be said as truly, though with less malice, that although they were in the twentieth century, they were never part of it, however enlightened or progressive they may have believed themselves to be.

We are not concerned here, however, with the sort of picture the Edwardians may have formed of themselves, a picture inevitably distorted by a lack of perspective; nor is there any intention of being either critical or didactic; the object is simply to show the Edwardians as they were – at work and at play, in the towns and in the country, the young, the middle aged and the old, the rich and the poor. Theirs was perhaps the last age of innocence, a time when the perfectability of man, however remote, could still have seemed believable; a time in which human beings were still recognized as more important than political theories; a time in which governments existed to serve the needs of their people, not people the needs of their governments; a time that would have had no truck with the illusions of the permissive society.

But let the pictures you are about to look at speak for themselves.

*'To each generation, that which preceded it*
*must seem in some measure,*
*according to its expectation of a hopeful futurity,*
*the last age of innocence.'*

Nathaniel Bigg

*A Discourse on the Faculty of Recollection.*

# Domestic Bliss

To have and to hold from this day forward,
for better, for worse,
for richer, for poorer,
in sickness and in health,
to love and to cherish,
till death us do part.

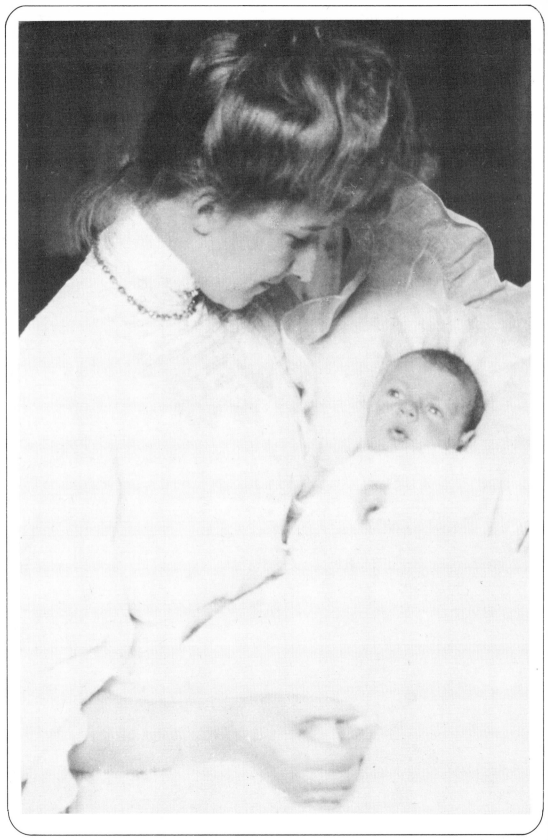

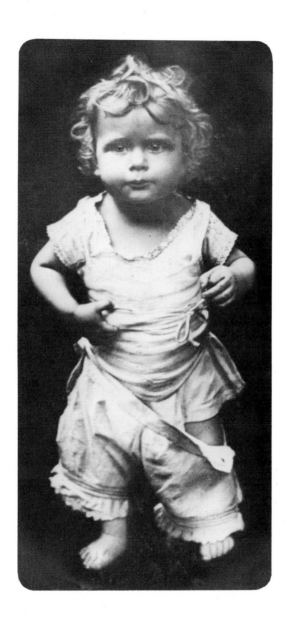

The world on which Edwardian infants gazed was a world that seemed to many
of their parents secure and immutable.
The inculcation of regular habits was a cardinal principle of Edwardian pediatrics.

'To all, to each, a fair goodnight,
And pleasing dreams and slumbers light.'

The deprived generation. Without television, without the cinema,
without even a transistor radio, the Edwardian child
was often faced with having nothing to do but read a book.

Goodbye, dolly, I must leave you.

The clothes that were thought suitable for children
made as few concessions to comfort or
convenience as the clothing of their parents.

Playing with soldiers had a topical interest for young boys,
for within living memory the British army had been in action
in Africa, India, China, Burma and other far-flung territories.

'So I said to her, I said, "Now, Miss Cynthia, if you don't behave . . ."'

The natural superiority of the male over the female sex
was a concept in which the Edwardians believed implicitly
and taught their children to respect.

The Edwardian breakfast was a ritual in which
little variation occurred and none was permitted in its fundamentals –
toast, marmalade, and silence.

Ladies of leisure, lacking the intellectual stimulus of bingo or doing the pools, idled away their afternoons in gossip.

Love me, love my dog.

Without hi-fi, tape-recorders or transistors the Edwardians had to make do with their own musical talents. But did Schumann, played on an upright piano and in cricket boots, sound less delightful to their ears than a cassette to ours?

# Unwillingly to School

Most schoolboys are limited in
their enthusiasm for the pursuit of learning,
and pupils at Emmanuel School
in south-west London
seemed to be no exception.
Or was it the sober convention of schoolboy clothing
that got them down?

The idea that a school should look something like a cross between a monastery and a gaol was inherited from the Victorians and must have conditioned the attitude of many Edwardians towards education.

Chemistry with its opportunities for producing weird
effects and peculiar smells was generally rated to be
more interesting than some other subjects.

The mysogynist. The Edwardian schoolboy's view of co-education, usually encouraged by parental example, was that it was only for softies.

Preparatory schools run by clergymen who had missed their vocation, and helped by wives who acted as matrons, inculcated a respect for Church and Empire, if for nothing else, as seems often to have been the case.

Some schools, more liberal in their ideas about learning, encouraged
independence of mind, but also respect for tradition. At Eton one
such tradition was wearing a button-hole on George III's birthday.

All work and no play makes Gwylym a dull boy.
It was permitted at some schools, such as this one in Wales,
to take your iron hoop or taw alley with you.

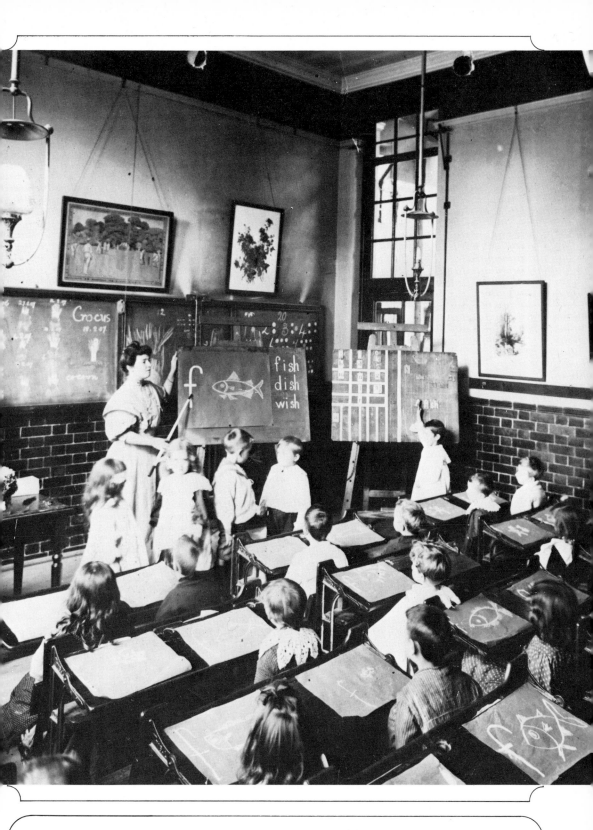

'F is for fish – yes, what is it you want, Cyril? . . . Very well, run along.'

Training was not confined to the intellect.
Here, at a north London girls' school, a class goes through
the motions of drill, under the Amazonian eye of the head-mistress.

And at this Chelsea school, in spite of restrictions on the
freedom of movement imposed by Edwardian notions of virgin modesty,
the young ladies enjoyed a spirited game of netball.

Domestic service, though among the worst-paid of occupations, provided
a variety of perks – such as living in – often lacking in better paid jobs,
so that girls could always be found who wanted to learn the skills of this kind of servitude.

Until you were old enough to have to face up to the real thing,
playing at schools was always fun.

# Travels and Excursions

A day's motoring in the country
was still something of a novelty in 1907;
so was the gear that was worn
for such an occasion.

The upper and middle classes travelled fairly freely.
Their journeys were usually for pleasure rather than for business reasons.
The rich and the more enterprising often went abroad, but the majority preferred

the familiar comforts of home to the dubious thrills and unknown perils
of the Continent. Most people travelled by one or other of the various railways —
AND had a porter to handle their luggage.

The masses could seldom afford to travel.
When they did so, it was probably to go on excursions at weekends or on Bank Holidays.
Members of society went to the time-honoured events that comprised their own

inviolable calendar. (*Left*): Kew Bridge station, Whit Monday, 1903:
the proletariat besieging trams bound for Hampton Court.
(*Right*): Ladies and gentlemen arriving at Henley-on-Thames for the Royal Regatta.

A day's outing in the park, with a trip on the lake thrown in, was also fun if you were the right age to enjoy it.

Or you could put your bicycle on the train
and then set off in search of adventure.

In Bath you could dash round the town in a Bath chair.
At Oxford you could go to the great fair held in St Giles in September (*overleaf*).

If you wanted to show you were really up-to-date, you could join
the Women's Aerial League, whose members met at Hendon aerodrome to applaud
and encourage those daring young men in their flying machines.

Foremost among these was the famous Claude Graham-White,
here seen risking life and limb in a 1911 Farman biplane.
Fortunately, he made a successful trip.

# Below Stairs

'*Dear Mum,*
  *I have got a good place*
*here with her Ladyship, though*
*the work is hard, six in*
*the morning till ten at night.*'

Housemaids learnt their job the hard way – under the watchful eye
of the housekeeper, herself probably a novice not so long ago,
and consequently the stricter for having survived the same routine.

A stitch in time saves a dressing-down by the mistress.

If it isn't washin' their bloomin' socks . . .
. . . it's ironin' their bloomin' shirts.

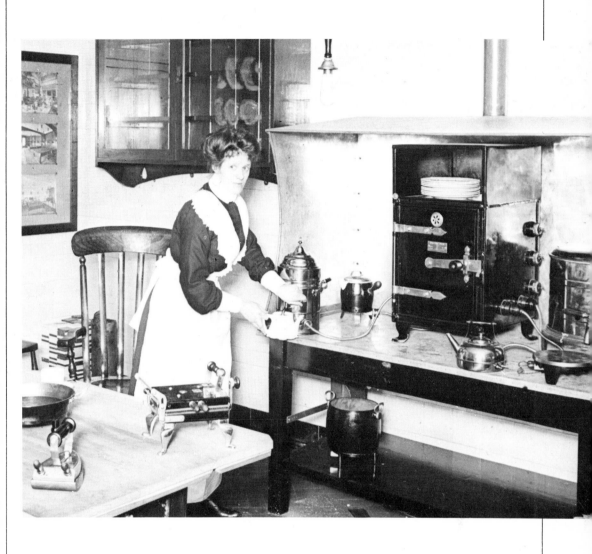

To be really advanced in 1908 meant having not only an
all-electric kitchen, but a parlourmaid who could master its equipment
without blowing the fuses or prostrating herself by a shock.

Below stairs Cook was the boss (and don't you forget it). She liked to run things her own way and as a rule didn't take readily to new-fangled devices.

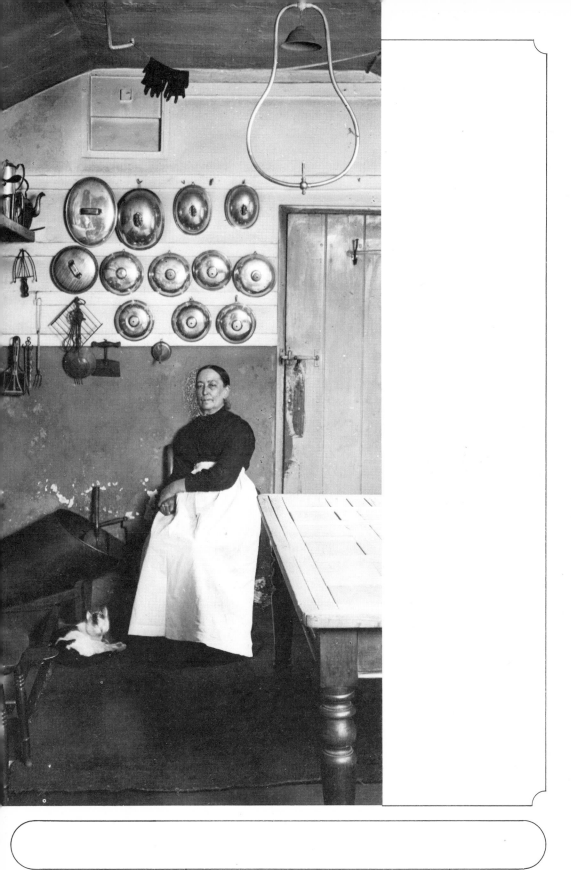

Sunday afternoon off.
Followers were usually discouraged by the mistress, but
not by the maid, especially on that weekly oasis of freedom, her half-day.

A nightcap for the party in the Private Room.

The ruling hierarchy of the male staff:
the groom, the coachman, and the butler.

Before long the duties of the coachman
were to be superseded by those of the chauffeur,
already in evidence at the car park at Ascot in 1907.

A breed apart were the gardeners.

The kennelman was also master of his own domain.

# London Life

Gone, all are gone, the old familiar places.
Romford Road, now one of London's busiest suburban thoroughfares,
as it was in 1908.

Gone, too, are some useful and once familiar characters. (*Left to right*): the drayman, who brought the British working man his beer; the butcher's boy, with his wooden trough, who delivered orders at the door;

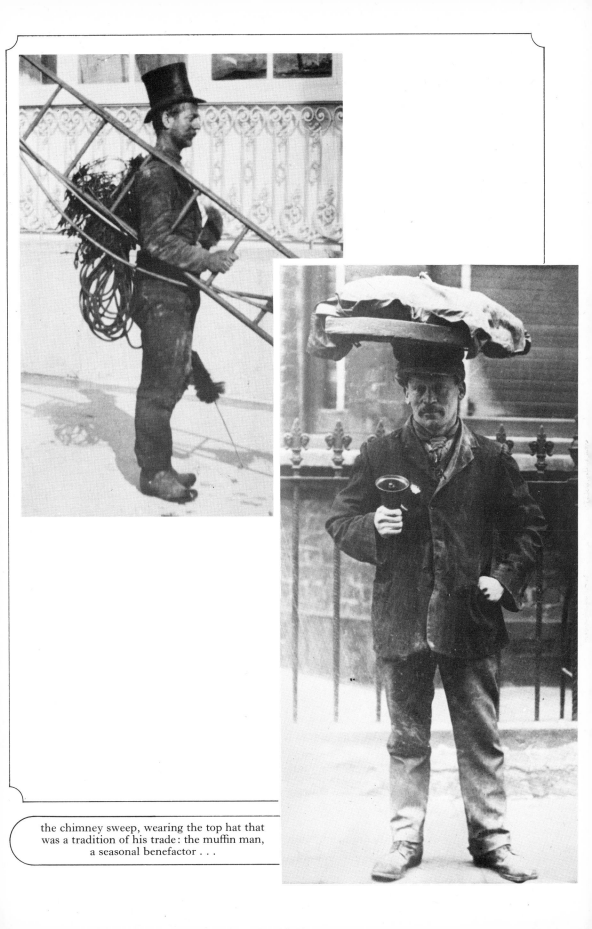

the chimney sweep, wearing the top hat that was a tradition of his trade: the muffin man, a seasonal benefactor . . .

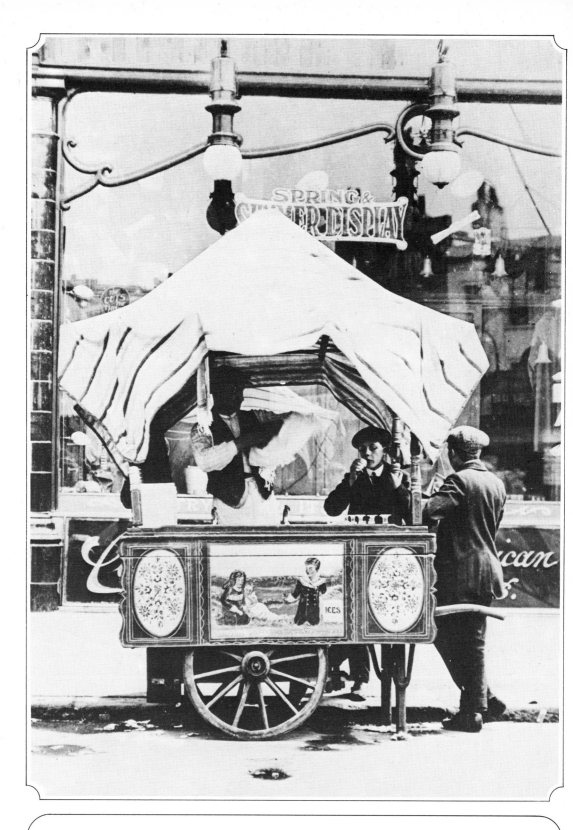

. . . the ice-cream or hokey-pokey merchant, a welcome sight on a hot day.

An attractive feature of the London scene, banished by bureaucracy
during the 1930s, were the flower sellers, whose pitches in Regent Street,
Piccadilly Circus and elsewhere, added gaiety to the streets.

By comparison with life in the suburbs, life in London was one unending rush.
The Strand, looking eastwards; on the left, St Clement Dane's church.

Things had begun to change in London's streets
with the coming of the motor omnibus,
the earliest of which were converted horse buses.

At about the same time, another means of transport,
the taxi cab, began to appear on the streets, and sometimes
proved to be the surest means of getting from place to place.

Which was not always so in a hansom cab. Fallen horses, although a not unusual sight,
appeared none the worse as a rule for having had a spill
and always seemed to attract an interested audience.

So, too, did the stars of musical comedy and the music hall:
Mabel Love (*above*), Lily Elsie, the original Merry Widow (*below*),
Little Tich (*opposite left*) and Harry Lauder (*opposite right*).

Huge crowds also went to the White City, a vast Anglo-Franco-Oriental
*fantaisie* improbably situated in Shepherd's Bush. It was the largest and most
spectacular show of its kind in Great Britain since the Great Exhibition of 1851.

Street music was always certain to attract a crowd.

Although the population of London was infinitely smaller than it is today, there usually seemed to be just as many people about, particularly in Oxford Street.

Many took their pick of the stalls in Wentworth Street
in the East End, where, as in other working-class districts,
life was a perpetual struggle to make both ends meet.

Charity bazaars to assist those engaged in the struggle provided
not only a certain amount of relief, but a chance for ladies
of fashion to show how deeply they felt for the deserving poor.

Such as those, for instance, who lived in Brewhouse Lane, Putney.

But there was another side to the coin: at Ashburton House
on Putney Heath they seemed to enjoy a measure of affluence that perhaps
gave them to think with compassion of their less fortunate neighbours.

# A Nation of Shopkeepers

That convenient and omnipresent Hermes,
the messenger boy on his tricycle,
has gone from our midst.

Increasing trade and commerce in the Edwardian period altered the appearance of many cities, necessitating their modernization and improvement. In some areas, such as Whitechapel, this meant the laying of tramway tracks.

Modernisation in Kingsway, the building of new office blocks. Property developers had already got their ravenous teeth into large slices of lucrative land.

Individual enterprise and a willingness to oblige seem to be becoming things of the past.
Before the advent of the chain-store and the supermarket they were
characteristic of thousands of provincial High Streets, such as St Botolph's, Colchester.

Before plastic packaging and the deep freeze, food could be made to look appetizing.
And for those who could afford it, there was always plenty of it.
Meat was usually Welsh or English – none of your New Zealand stuff.

On a busy weekday Piccadilly Circus looked rather different in 1910.

Whereas Embankment Gardens during the lunch hour
looked in some ways much the same as it does today.

Harrods' grocery department has always had an unrivalled reputation;
only its appearance seems to have changed.

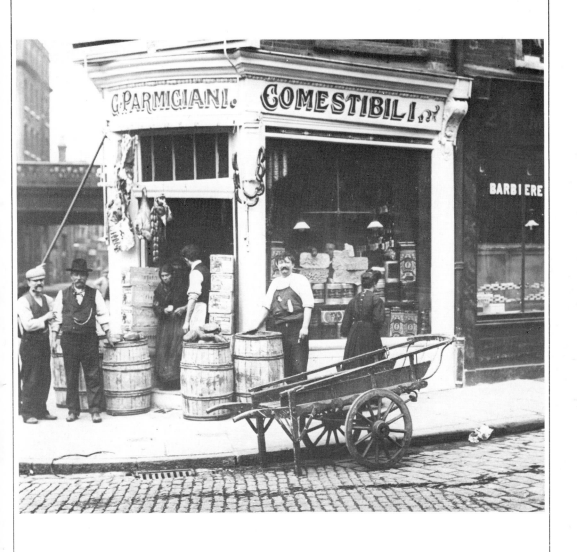

Not Naples, but Clerkenwell, where the Italian colony,
one of several such enclaves in various parts of London,
provided for itself the familiar comforts of home.

'I must just pop into the tailor.'
The august establishment of Poole's in Savile Row, by whom
most of the crowned heads of Europe were dressed.

It pays to advertise.

# In the Country

*'Can'st thou draw out Leviathan with thy hook?'*
Job, xli, 1.

'The harvest truly is plenteous, but the labourers are few.' Yet, toiling early and late, they achieved prodigious results, though most of the benefits of mechanized farming were still undeveloped.

The cottager's life was hard, making him largely self-sufficient.
Without any of today's numerous labour-saving gadgets he and his family
somehow seemed to understand the meaning of contentment.

The needy knife-grinder, gone, alas, the way of the tinker,
the chair-mender and other itinerant artisans without
whose skills the countryman is nowadays often the poorer.

'Everybody can see that the people who hunt are the right
people, and the people who don't are the wrong ones.'
Bernard Shaw, *Heartbreak House*.

An outing of the Camera Club at Burnham Beeches in Buckinghamshire.
Even before the days of the wide-angled lens and the panchromatic film,
the woods in autumn were a tempting sight to photographers.

But the camera is no substitute for
the vision of the artist and, of course,
can't get you into the Royal Academy.

That well-fed feeling.
Edwardian picnics were more than mere snacks;
good solid food was expected – and drink.

Fetching water from a communal well was
in some places a customary chore, but it usually gave
a chance of adding to the stock of village gossip.

So did a chat with the postman.
Or with your pals after the day's work. Village alehouses had none of the synthetic,
plastichrome atmosphere of the modern pub, but a pint of old and mild still tasted good.

LOST – and not a soul in sight. Mixed bicycling was an
innocent enterprise, but not without its hazards when
everyone had different views about which way to go.

# The Seaside

The novelty of feeling sand
between the toes
was all part of the fun.

Going to the seaside was by far
the most popular form of holiday,
both among grown-ups and children.

For the young it was an unaccustomed pleasure
and for the old a welcome change of circumstance.

There was always something to do that you couldn't do at home.
You could go on the pier, for instance . . . or listen to the pierrots.

Small fry could enjoy the thrill of driving in a goat cart . . . or could watch the Punch and Judy show.

Not exactly a quick dip. It was sometimes a dashed nuisance
having to wait such ages on the jetty, and then there was often
a long haul to the bathing machines.

But it was, oh, so jolly when you got into the water!

You could also swap yarns about boating
(probably on the Serpentine or the lake in Regent's Park)
with some of the old salts.

A Proustian moment on the Isle of Wight . . .
. . . perhaps leading to an acquaintance.

Best of all was the sheer pleasure of just getting your feet wet.

# The Sporting Life

They're off!
The sport of kings has always attracted commoners
as well as crowned heads. Ascot races, 1907.

Cricket, though perhaps less of a fetish than it has since become,
was almost as much a ritual as a game. Worcester *versus* the Australians at
Worcester in 1905. At the end of an exciting match spectators surge onto the pitch.

Wimbledon, 1908.
A thrilling ladies' doubles has the spectators
on the edge of their seats.

A tear-away start in the relay race at Brooklands, Surrey.
Motor racing, although in its infancy,
was already becoming popular as early as 1909.

Ballooning was another sport in which
there was considerable public interest.
Getting airborne was not always easy.

But, oh, the peace of being aloft!

At the Olympic Games in 1908, held at the White City stadium, new time and distance records were set up, though these have since been far exceeded. *Above :* undeterred by British summer weather, a packed crowd watches the 100 kilometre bicycle race.

Erik Lemming, of Sweden, smashing the javelin-throwing record
with a pitch of 53.90 metres. The present record, set up in 1968
at the Mexico Games by J. Lusis, of the USSR, is 90.10 metres.

Henry Taylor, winner of two gold medals for Great Britain in swimming events,
broke the 1500 metres free-style record with a time of 22 minutes 48 seconds.
At Munich in 1972 the time for the same race was 15.37 minutes.

Forrest Smithson (second from right), of the United States,
won a gold medal in the 110 metres hurdles with a record time of 15 seconds.
The existing record was cut to 13.2 seconds at Munich.

A gold medal was also won for the United States by Martin Sheridan,
who threw the discus 42.63 metres in his suspenders!
The present record, set up at Mexico in 1968, is 68.40 metres.

In the 1500 metres race N. W. Sheppeard, United States, set up
a new Olympic record with a time of 4.03 minutes. Today's world record,
held by James Ryun, also of the United States, is 3 minutes 33.1 seconds.

Denmark's team of women gymnasts performed hair-raising feats on the horizontal bar.

In the pole vault Ed Archibald, of Canada, watched by a somewhat
limited audience, jumped 3.58 metres. The record, set up by R. Seagram,
United States, at Mexico, stands at 5.40 metres.

In the 10-mile walk (now discontinued), George Larner, Great Britain,
achieved a record time of 1 hour 15.57 minutes.

Bowls at the Crystal Palace: a cliff-hanger in the final match of the day.

The royal and ancient game of golf had taken on a new
lease of life in the '90s, and now among several popular players was
Ted Ray, here seen driving off, with a stance that seems all his own.

The last race at Ascot leaves one attractive filly unplaced.

# The Beginning of the End

The King is dead. Long live the King. On May 6, 1910 King Edward died.
So started the decline of a way of life that Englishmen would never know again.
Its *coup de grâce* came in 1914 with the outbreak of the Great War.

Black Ascot. As no doubt the late King would have wished,
as few changes as possible were made in public arrangements.

A few weeks after his death the Ascot race meeting took place
as usual, with the spectators wearing mourning.

In the following year, the coronation of George V brought to
London thousands of spectators, many in special omnibuses, to
see the procession and cheer their new king.

When the war came, three years later, recruiting offices were swamped
with volunteers. They responded to the call with the traditional good humour
of the British, but for many of them this was their last laugh.

*Soldiers are dreamers; when the guns begin*
   *They think of firelit homes, clean beds, and wives.*
*I see them in foul dug-outs, gnawed by rats,*
   *And in the ruined trenches, lashed with rain,*
*Dreaming of things they did with balls and bats,*
   *And mocked by hopeless longing to regain*
*Bank-holidays, and picture-shows, and spats,*
   *And going to the office in the train.*

     From *Dreamers* by Siegfried Sassoon.

# Bibliography

# Photographic
# Acknowledgements

# Index

# Bibliography

Anon. *The Duties of Servants,* Warne, n.d.

Bott, Alan, *Our Fathers,* Heinemann, 1931.

Clive, Mary, *The Day of Reckoning,* Macmillan, 1964.

Leslie, Anita, *Edwardians in Love,* Hutchinson, 1972.

Magnus, Philip, *King Edward the Seventh,* Murray and E. P. Dutton & Co., Inc., New York, 1964.

Middlemas, Keith, *The Life and Times of Edward VII,* Weidenfeld and Nicolson and Doubleday & Company, Inc., New York, 1972.

Peel, Mrs C. S., *How to Keep House,* Constable, 1902.

Plowden, William, *The Motor Car and Politics, 1896–1970,* Bodley Head, 1971.

Reed, Donald, *Edwardian England, Documents from Edwardian England,* Harrap, 1973.

Reeves, Mrs Pember, *Round About a Pound a Week,* Bell, 1913.

Sackville-West, V., *The Edwardians,* Hogarth Press, 1930.

Sykes, Christopher, *Four Studies in Loyalty,* Collins and Sloan & Co., New York, 1946.

Thompson, Flora, *Lark Rise to Candleford : A Trilogy,* Oxford University Press, London and New York, 1945.

Wells, H. G., *Experiment in Autobiography,* Gollancz, and Macmillan, Inc., New York, 1934.

# Photographic Acknowledgements

The photographs in this book were collected by Mrs Andra Nelki, who together with the publishers, would particularly like to thank the large number of people who showed them pictures in their private family albums. A number of these were copied by Geoff Goode for reproduction in this book.

The photographs used are reproduced by kind permission of the following:

Aerofilms Ltd: 3, 15 *bottom*, 98/99, 157, 173, 174, 176 *bottom*, 177 *top*, 178/179, 181, 202/203

Barnabys Picture Library: 114, 182 *bottom*

Bassano & Vandyke Studios: 23 *top right*, 51 *top right*

Camera Press: 212/213

The Couzins & Powney Collection: 80, 82/83, 101, 123, 150, 163, 175, 182 *top*

Richard Dennis Collection: 13, 45, 84, 183

Baron de Veauce: 74/75

Mrs H. Dobbie: 64

Mrs J. R. Ede: 73, 77, 93, 119

Flight International: 104, 105, 189

William Gordon Davis: 44, 65, 125 *right*, 134 *top*, 134 *bottom*, 135 *right*

Greater London Council Photograph Library: 28, 41, 46, 81, 86, 87, 89, 90, 108, 112/113, 146/147, 148/149

Guildhall: 124 *top*, 124 *bottom*, 207

Harrods: 154

Howarth-Loomes Collection: 180

Mrs O. N. Jeffcock: 115, 120/121

Kodak Museum: 9, 12 *top*, 15 *top*, 30 *bottom*, 34 *top*, 39 *bottom*, 61, 66, 67, 68, 70, 72, 109, 110 *top*, 110 *bottom*, 125 *left*, 166, 170/171, 176 *top*

London Museum: 26, 27 *bottom*

London Transport Executive: 96, 130, 131, 145, 210

Mrs H. MacColl and Miss P. H. Bruce: 69

Kevin MacDonnell: 30 *top*, 36/37, 91, 159, 162, 165, 168, 169 *bottom*

The Raymond Mander and Joe Mitchenson Theatre Collection: 12 *bottom*, 14, 55

Mansell Collection: 17, 21, 31 *top*, 31 *middle*, 51 *bottom right*, 51 *bottom left*, 135 *left*

Mirror Pic: 211

National Motor Museum: 152

National Portrait Gallery: 51 *middle*

Olney Collection: Mr Peter Gerhold and Mr D. C. Harrod: 48, 63, 79, 138, 142, 143

Henry Poole and Co Ltd, Savile Row: 156

Popperfoto: 23 *bottom right*

Press Association: 191, 192, 193, 194/195, 196, 197, 198/199, 200, 201, 204

Radio Times Hulton Picture Library: 18, 19, 22, 23 *top left*, 23 *bottom left*, 24 *top*, 24 *bottom*, 31 *bottom*, 32, 34 *bottom*, 35, 49, 51 *top left*, 53, 54, 57, 58, 59, 71, 76, 85, 88, 94, 95, 100, 102/103, 103, 107, 111, 116, 117, 118, 126, 127, 136/137, 139, 140, 141, 151 *top*, 151, *bottom*, 153, 155, 164, 167, 185, 186, 187, 188, 205, 208/209

Royal Aeronautical Society: 190

# Index

Agricultural labour, 38–9
Albert Hall, 29
Alexandra, Queen, 18, 20
Alma-Tadema, Sir Laurence, 52
Amalgamated Society of Railway Servants, 38
Archibald, Ed, 200
Army Medical Service, 42
Arne, Thomas, 55
Arnold Matthew, 17
Ascot Races, 117, 185, 205, 208–9
Ashburton House, Putney Heath, 143
Asquith, Rt. Hon. Henry Herbert (1st Earl of
    Oxford and Asquith), 22, 23, 25, 27, 29, 60
Auden, Wystan Hugh, 56
Automobile Club, 34, 35

Balfe, Michael William, 55
Balfour, Rt. Hon. Arthur James (1st Earl of), 22,
    23, 24, 25, 29
Ballinslaughter Hill Climb, 34
*Barrack-room Ballads* (Kipling), 13
Barrie, Sir James, 52
Bath, Somerset, 101
Beaconsfield, Earl of, *see* Disraeli
Beckett, Samuel, 56
Beeton, Mrs Isabella, 47
Bennett, Arnold, 52
Bigg, Nathaniel, *quoted*, 61
Bismarck, Prince von, 24
Boulter's Lock, Middlesex, 59
Booth, Charles, 40
Bourne, Cardinal, Archbishop of Westminster,
    31
Brett, Hon. Maurice, 17
Brewhouse Lane, Putney, 142
Brooklands, motor racing at, 188
Buckingham Palace, 27, 58
Buller, Sir Redvers, 11
Burnham Beeches, Bucks, 165
Busvine, Messrs, 33

Caine, Sir Hall, 51
Camden Town Group, 54
Camera Club, 165

Cameron, Julia, 15
Campbell-Bannerman, Sir Henry, 22, 23, 25, 27,
    29
Campion, Thomas, 55
Chartism, 42; Chartist manifesto (1838), 26, 27
Chesterton, Gilbert Keith, 52
Chisholm, Hugh, *quoted*, 21
Churchill, Rt Hon. Sir Winston, 23, 24, 25, 27,
    29
Church of England, 11, 17, 20, 31
Clerkenwell, London, 155
Clifford, Dr John, 31
Cobden, Richard, 26
Coldstream Guards, 17
Collier, Hon. John, 52, 54
Commons, House of, 11, 25
Conservative party, 11
Corelli, Marie, 17, 51
Crystal Palace, Sydenham, 57, 203
Cup Final, Football Association, 57

Daly's Theatre, 42
Dare, Miss Zena (Hon. Mrs Maurice Brett), 17
Davidson, Randall, Archbishop of Canterbury,
    31
*Defence of Philosophy, A* (Balfour), 24
De Morgan, William, 49
Derby Stakes, 20, 57
Dickens, Charles, 42, 43
Dicksee, Sir Francis, 53, 54
Disraeli, Benjamin (Earl of Beaconsfield), 24, 26
Domestic service, 43, 45–8
Dowland, John, 55
Downing Street, No. 10, 27
Drummond, Mrs Elsie, 27
Drury Lane Theatre, 14

Education Act (1902), 11
Edward VII, King, 11, 12, 17, 18, 21, 22, 23, 24,
    25, 27, 29, 33, 43, 44, 50, 51, 57, 60, 207,
    208–9
*Edwardian England* (Read), 41
Elgar, Sir Edward, 55
Elsie, Lily, 134

Emmanuel School, Wandsworth, 79
Entente Cordiale, 21
Eton College, 85
Eton and Harrow cricket match, 58, 59
Esher, Reginald, 2nd Viscount, 17, 21 *quoted*

Fallières, President Armand, 18
Farquharson, Joseph, 53, 54
First World War, 29, 45, 60, 207
Fisher, Admiral of the Fleet, Sir John (Lord
    Fisher of Kilverstone), 21
Ford, Thomas, 55
*Foundations of Belief* (Balfour), 24

Gaiety Theatre, 42
Galsworthy, John, 52
Garvice, Charles, 51
George III's birthday celebrated at Eton, 85
George V, King, 11, 21, 210
Germanic states, unification of, 24
Gilman, Harold, 54
Gladstone, Rt. Hon. William Ewart, 26, 50, 60
Glasgow Exhibition of Decorative and Industrial
    Art (1901), 49
Glover, James, 14
Glyn, Elinor, 17, 51
Golden Mile, Henley Royal Regatta, 59
Golders Green, Middlesex, 49
Goncourt brothers, 42
Gordon-Cumming, Lieut-Col. Sir William, 20
Gore, Spencer, 54
Gould, Nat, 51
Graham-White, Claude, 105
Grand Challenge Cup, Henley Royal Regatta, 59
Great Exhibition (1851), 50, 137
Great War, *see* First World War
Grey, Sir Edward (Viscount Grey of Falloden),
    27
Grosvenor Chapel, Mayfair, 33
*Guide to the Turf,* Ruff's, 24

Haggard, Sir Rider, 52
Hampton Court, Middlesex, 97
Hardy, Thomas, 52
Harris, Frank, 52
Harrods, Messrs, 154
Hartmann, Mrs James, 43
Health and physique of the people, Committee
    on, 42
Hendon aerodrome, 104
Henley Royal Regatta, 59, 97
Highbury football stadium, 58
Hill, David Octavius, 15
Hilliard, Nicholas, 52
Hitchens, Robert, 51
Hogarth, William, 52
Holloway Gaol, 27
Hope (Hawkins, Sir) Anthony, 51
*Household Management* (Beeton), 47
Howie, Miss Elsie, 27

*How to Keep House* (Peel), 45, 46
Huxley, Aldous, 56
Hyde Park, London, 20, 32, 33

Ibsen, Henrik, 17
Industrial Revolution, 16
Ireland, problem of, 11

Jay's, Messrs, 16
James, Henry, 52
Johnson, Claude, 34–5
Joyce, James, 56

Keppel, Hon. Mrs George, 20, 43
Kew Bridge, Middlesex, 97
Keyser, Sister Agnes, 43
Kingsway, London, 148–9
Kipling, Rudyard, 12, 52, 59
Kitchener of Khartoum, 1st Earl, 11, 12
Klee, Paul, 56

Labour Party, 27, 38
Lambeth, London, 35
Langtry, Lillie (Lady de Bathe), 19, 20, 43
Larner, George, 201
Latimer, Bishop Hugh, 29
Lauder, Sir Harry, 135
Law, Rt Hon. Andrew Bonar, 27
Leeds, Yorks, 41
Léger, Fernand, 56
Leighton, Frederick, Baron, 53
Lemming, Erik, 192
Leslie, Anita, *quoted*, 54
Liberal Party, 29
*Life and Labour of the People of London* (Booth), 40
Little Tich (Harry Relph), 135
Lloyd George, David (1st Earl), 24, 25, 29
Local Government Board, 33
Lords Cricket Ground, 58; members' stand, 59
Lords, House of, 11, 38; reform of, 25
Love, Mabel, 134
Lusis, J., 192
Lutyens, Sir Edwin, 50

Mackintosh, Rennie, 50
Magnus, Philip, *quoted*, 17, 19, 43
Marble Arch, 33
Mass Observation, 38
Maugham, William Somerset, 52
Maxwell, William Babington, 52
Mayhew, Henry, 38
Melbourne, 2nd Viscount, 24
Merrick, Leonard, 51
Middlemas, Keith, *quoted*, 25
Mill, John Stuart, 26
Minoru, 21
Modigliani, Amadeo, 56
Morris, William, 48
Morton, J. B., *quoted*, 12
*Motor Car and Politics, The* (Plowden), 33

Northcliffe, 1st Baron, 26

Olympic Games, White City (1908), 191, 192,
    193, 194–5, 196–9, 200, 201;
    Mexico City (1968), 192, 196, 200;
    Munich (1972), 193, 194
Oval cricket ground, Lambeth, 58
Oxford Street, London, 139

Pankhurst, Mrs Emmeline, 26, 27, 29
Parliament Bill (1910), 11
Peel, Mrs Dorothy, 45, *quoted*, 46–7
Picasso, Pablo, 56
Piccadilly Circus, 127, 152
Plowden, William, *quoted*, 33, 34
Poole, Messrs Henry, and Co., 156
*Poverty : A Study of Town Life* (Rowntree), 40
Poynter, Sir Edward, 53
Purcell, Henry, 55
Pre-Raphaelite Brotherhood, 52

Queen's Hall Promenade Concerts, 55

Ray, Ted, 204
Read, Donald, *quoted*, 41
Redfern, Messrs, 33
Reeves, Mrs Pember, *quoted*, 35–6, 38, 40
Reform Bill (1884), 26, 31, 43
Regent Street, London, 127
Ridley, Bishop Nicholas, 29
Rita, 51
Rivière, Briton, 53
Roberts, Field-Marshal Earl, 11, 12
Rotten Row, Hyde Park, 32, 33
Rowntree, Seebohm, 41, 42
*Round About a Pound a Week* (Reeves), 35–6
Royal Academy, 52, 53
Ryun, James, 197

St Botolph's, Colchester,
St Clement Dane's Church, Strand, 178
St George's Church, Hanover Square, 33
St Giles Fair, Oxford, 102–3
St James's Church, Piccadilly, 33
Salisbury, 3rd Marquess of, 22, 23, 24
Sant, James, 53
Sargent, John Singer, 54
Sassoon, Siegfried, *quoted*, 212
Savile Row, London, 156
Seagram, R., 200
Serpentine Lake, Regent's Park, 181
Shaw, George Bernard, 11, 13, 17, 52, *quoted*,
    164
Shaw, Norman, 50
Sheffield, Yorks, 41
Sheridan, Martin, 196
Sheppeard, N. W., 197
Sickert, Walter Richard, 52, 54

Sitwell, Dame Edith, *quoted*, 17
Sitwell, Sir Osbert, *quoted*, 55
Smiles, Samuel, 17
Smithson, Forrest, 194
*Soul's Awakening, The* (Sant), 53
Soviet regime, 18
Speed limit, 33
Stanford, Sir Charles Villiers, 55
Stone, Marcus, 53, 54
Stubbs, George, 52
Suffragettes, 11, 26, 27, 29
Sullivan, Sir Arthur, 55
Sutherland, Graham, 54
Swears and Wells, Messrs, 16
Sykes, Christopher, 20

Taff Vale Railway Company, and judgement, 38
Talbot, Fox, 15
Tariff reform, 11
Taylor, Henry, 193
Thackeray, William Makepeace, 42
Thurston, Ernest Temple, 52
Tolpuddle Martyrs, 38
Trade Disputes Act (1906), 38
Trade disputes and combinations, Royal
    Commission on, 38
Tranby Croft affair, 20
Trollope, Anthony, 42
Tupper, Martin, 17
Turner, James William Mallord, 52

Unionist Party, 29

Victoria, Queen, 11, 14, 17, 21, 24, 43, 50
Votes for Women, 26, 27, 29
Voysey, C. F. A., 50

Warwick, 6th Earl of, 45
Warwick, Frances, Countess of, 43, 45
Wells, Herbert George, 11, 52
Welwyn Garden City, Herts, 49
Wentworth Street, London, 140
Whistler, James McNeil, 52
Whitechapel, 147
White City exhibition, 18, 136–7; stadium, 191
Wilhelm II, Kaiser, 17, 42
Wilson, Richard, 52
Wimbledon, Lawn Tennis Association's meeting
    at, 187
Woking, Surrey, 58
Wolseley, Field-Marshal Viscount, 11, 12
Women's Aerial League, 104
Women's Social and Political Union, 26
Wood, Sir Henry, 55, 56
Worcester Country Cricket Club, 186
Worth, Charles Frederick, 33

Yeats, William Butler, 52
York, 40